Welcoming Marriage

Welcoming Marriage

A practical and pastoral guide to the new legislation

Stephen Lake

CHURCH HOUSE
PUBLISHING

Church House Publishing
Church House
Great Smith Street
London SW1P 3AZ

Tel: 020 7898 1451
Fax: 020 7898 1449

ISBN 978–0–7151–4172–4

Published 2009 by Church House Publishing

The opinions expressed in this book are those of
the individual authors and do not necessarily
reflect the official policy of the General Synod or
The Archbishops' Council of the Church of England.

Typeset in 9.5pt Stone Sans
by RefineCatch Limited, Bungay, Suffolk
Printed by Ashford Colour Press Ltd, Fareham, Hants

Contents

Acknowledgements

This book began on the floor of General Synod when, having voted through the Marriage Measure, it was immediately clear to me that something would be needed to help the Church make the most of this new mission initiative. Time was short and the swift passage of the legislation through Parliament made the task more immediate. To that end I am in the debt of those who helped me produce *Welcoming Marriage*.

Kathryn Pritchard, Commissioning and Product Development Manager at Church House Publishing, who has been an inspiration and a critical friend, while keeping it all a fun thing to do.

Lynda Barley, Head of Research and Statistics for the Archbishops' Council, for writing Chapter 3 and for making sense of this valuable research.

Christopher Jones, Home Affairs Policy Adviser to the Archbishops' Council, for his clarity and contribution to Chapter 4.

Peter Moger, National Worship Development Officer, for his liturgical insight and priestly advice.

Sue Burridge, Policy Adviser on Marriage and Family to the Archbishops' Council for her assistance with Chapter 2.

Gillian Oliver, Project Manager for the Weddings Project for training and for working in partnership.

Paul Bayes, National Mission and Evangelism Adviser, for believing in the project.

Tim Sledge, Vicar of Romsey Abbey and Rhiannon Jones, Rector of Fulbourn and the Wilbrahams, for their wedding stories.

Maggie York, my assistant at St Alban's Cathedral, for welcoming so many couples.

Finally, I dedicate *Welcoming Marriage* to all those couples I have had the pleasure and privilege to marry over the last 20 years, and most especially to Carol, still my bride today.

Stephen Lake

Introduction

It's lunchtime on Saturday. I'm just catching the end of *Football Focus*. It's time to go really but I just want to see what the pundits are predicting about today's results. So running five minutes late I walk purposefully across to the cathedral for the wedding that I'm taking in 25 minutes' time – just enough time to ensure everything is in place for the match of the day. A couple are waiting for me. Not *the* couple but another young couple that I haven't met before. The vergers have said I'd be the one they need to talk to about getting married. I haven't really got the time. I should have left earlier.

Yet their faces say it all. Their story is familiar, I've heard it all before, but here they are, in love, excited, nervous, hypersensitive about their circumstances. It's a big moment, here they are standing in an English cathedral, in front of a priest, asking if they can get married. With the urgency of the fast-approaching service in the forefront of my mind, the nature of my response will colour all future conversations and even how they feel about the Church. More than that, this moment also sums up in an instant how God feels about them and their love for each other. Something has brought them to this point, something has stirred within them to want a church wedding, and hurried comments from me about where they live and fees are not going to inspire them. This brief encounter is loaded with importance and potential for growth and yet also potential for disappointment.

The Church of England has recently changed the rules for marriage qualification. This is not solely to combat falling numbers of church weddings, although some may view these changes in this way. The new marriage legislation reflects more fully the needs of today and the way in which couples present themselves for marriage before God. In a fast-changing world, the church can seem slow to react. The Church must balance need with principle and, in England, with the requirements of legislation also. Yet in this new legislation, now in force, there is the opportunity for greater hospitality and mission in the administration of holy matrimony.

Welcoming Marriage is a handbook to guide clergy, ordinands and parish representatives through these changes and to encourage really good practice. The liturgical, pastoral and teaching opportunities can be maximized to make weddings uniquely special, as special to the Church as to each and every couple. The challenge and the responsibility for church leaders is to ensure that every wedding is a 'mission moment'. And even though a wedding is a single event, the Church's approach to that wedding is symbolic of the inestimable value of marriage that is both lifelong and a blessing to society. God can indeed work through our professional ministry in this vital area and he is calling us in Christ to a greater, deeper and more open engagement with couples.

The wedding started on time and the service was watched by the enquiring new couple. Over a coffee in the Refectory after the service, time was given and clear information shared. The way forward for this couple was explained and received with understanding and with joy. And I was still back home in plenty of time for *Final Score*. For both couples, life would never be the same again; the Church was indeed welcoming their marriage.

Welcoming Marriage includes:

- new understandings of weddings today;

- the background to this legislative change;

- how the new framework for marriage qualification will work;

- detailed research on the motivations and barriers for couples to marry in church;

- good practice for clergy and parishes in welcoming couples;

- teaching examples for clergy with couples;

- how to celebrate the liturgy of marriage in church really well;

- marriage as mission;

- resources and future developments in the Church.

The task of the Church is to respond enthusiastically to these changes and challenges, for in so doing, we share in the ministry of Christ himself.

> A wedding is one of life's great moments, a time of solemn commitment as well as good wishes, feasting and joy. St John tells us how Jesus shared in such an occasion at Cana, and gave there a sign of new beginnings as he turned water into wine.
>
> *Common Worship: Pastoral Services*, Pastoral Introduction[1]

1

Weddings today

How do today's couples approach the whole process of getting married, what if any are their expectations of the Church and what does this mean for those of us who minister in this area? This chapter looks at the world of weddings today and the market-place that is now taken for granted by couples. What are the influences upon couples and how do they make their decisions around their 'special day'? What are the ways in which the Church can respond effectively, pastorally and wholeheartedly to their love for one another?

Are you a real vicar?

The telephone rang. I picked it up and it was the Communications Department of the Church of England. They wanted a couple of 'cute' clergy to staff a stall at a national wedding fair. At the cathedral there were no cute canons so the task fell to the younger (and cuter) minor canons. Now, we don't get out much in cathedral life, most of us experience a sense of liberation when we are allowed out to visit the local supermarket, so the chance of a corporate day out was enthusiastically embraced.

The day arrived and our two minor canons tripped off, trying to look their best. They were entering unknown territory. Theological College had not prepared them for this – apart from having to write an essay on Daniel in the lions' den. They were entering the whole new world of weddings today and, although they had something distinctive to offer, they were uncertain to what extent they would be out of place. Just to be on the safe side and blend in, they wore their cassocks!

The wedding fair was vast, held at one of the national arenas. Entering the market-place felt strange, not the usual method of engagement with the world of weddings for the Church of England. There was an amusing juxtaposition of the stalls. The Church of England stall was next to one for wedding cakes and opposite the one for *Buff Brides* – personal trainers for today's bride-to-be. Next came the company offering pole dancing for hen nights and another selling bikinis and sarongs for the best-dressed guests at your Caribbean beach wedding.

As couples came and went, the one question people kept asking the two priests was, 'Are you a real vicar?' Many people seemed to think they were a spoof from central casting. However, what they found hardest to grasp, was that, alone out of all the exhibitors, these two ministers were not trying to sell anything. How could something, let alone something special, be available for no more than statutory fees? People were bemused that the Church was there simply to offer help and advice, and was genuinely pleased for them, whether they were having a church wedding or not. In order to clinch the deal, the minor canons handed round fair trade chocolate!

Some couples could not get rid of the preconception that these two clergy *should* be selling something. For many, weddings are a commercial product and you make your choice as a couple of consumers, according to your pocket and your personal preferences. Everyone else at the fair had a product and if it was worth having it was going to cost a lot of money.

Interestingly, many people thought that church weddings cost more and were for churchy people only. So, what couples seemed to find most striking was that the priests had time for them and were happy to offer simple, honest advice, even offering to pray for them in the months ahead. Couples seemed surprised and grateful for this. With the aid of a computer link, couples were advised of their parish church and of how to get in touch with their incumbent. It also became clear that most people were bemused by the legalities around weddings, and for many, this proved to be a stumbling block. Knowledge of these legalities was patchy at best and many still found it complicated and difficult to understand, even after explanation. Everyone else here was trying to get them in, not turn them away to somewhere else. So, although when given help and encouragement many couples were open to the possibility of a church wedding, few had arrived at the wedding fair feeling informed or welcome enough to make this a positive choice.

Church in the market-place

This true account reflects the new way in which weddings are viewed today by those planning for marriage. It is in this context that the Church must function and communicate the vital and distinctive character of Christian marriage. The Church must see this new context as an opportunity rather than a retrograde development. Either we believe we have something special to offer in the competitive weddings market or we are just an outdated expression of cultural practice. If we believe in the value of a wedding in church to begin a marriage, we need to be sure we are embodying this confident belief in every contact, every exchange of information and every description of what marriage is, in both practical and spiritual terms. We must be proud of what we offer couples, for, through our words and actions, Christ can make his home with them in their new life together.

The new legislation for marriages in church gives us this mission opportunity and the pastoral responsibility to exercise this vital ministry with renewed professionalism and flair.

So weddings are now big business and as with any big business the market-place is vibrant and challenging. In the past couples had a limited choice between the wedding in the local church or a civil ceremony in the local Register Office. Now their choice is almost endless, with stunning venues competing for their attention. Weddings are the subject of advertising, promotions and special package deals and can be celebrated at an ever-growing list of unique venues at home and abroad.

A few years ago a friend of mine was on sabbatical in our linked diocese and his family stayed at a hotel in Antigua for a week's holiday. Several times a day they were disturbed by the 'wedding chapel' taped music as couples arrived for their all-inclusive wedding ceremony, with witnesses thrown in from the table waiting staff if you couldn't afford to fly the family out. Each ceremony lasted just seven minutes but the backdrop of the Caribbean framed by palm trees was second to none. Quite apart from the view, the attraction of a tropical wedding and honeymoon thrown into one package with reception included has its appeal for some.

Few Church of England parishes can offer the same in vista or facilities for the party. Church halls don't really compete. We are just not used to functioning in this competitive environment.

Traditionally, couples came to us because the Church held what amounted almost to a monopoly. That is one of the reasons why rules for qualification exist, to find a way of managing marriage applications in a fair and parish-based way. But most couples live today as part of the Internet generation with flexible access to consumer services, information and mobility as a given. Parish boundaries and the historic sense of community become increasingly meaningless to those wishing to be married today. Everyone they come into contact with regarding their marriage is offering choice (at a price). In contrast, the Church has, typically, offered questions around the topic of suitability and what can easily feel like interrogation.

Recently, an adult confirmation candidate of a local parish priest was growing really well as a Christian. But when it came to her marriage, the lure of the castle with flaming torches lining the long drive to the door meant that a wedding in church just did not enter her thinking. Guests

could come to the one dramatic venue and stay the night
so that the celebration of the whole event could be
prolonged with an evening party till the small hours,
followed by reflective breakfast concluding with departure
by helicopter from the castle lawn. From her perspective,
there was no competition.

So, the vicar is no longer the first port of call following the marriage
proposal. The Internet is there for first reference. Web sites such as
confetti.co.uk or WeddingGuideUK.com or hitched.co.uk or
magic-dust.co.uk are often the place that couples will discover their
initial information about getting married. Marriage insurance is on offer
just as one might take out holiday or pet insurance. And if all this is too
much, why not engage the services of a wedding planner, someone to
take the cares and concerns out of the arrangements so that the couple
can sit back and enjoy the whole event in a carefree and client-based
relationship?

Clearly, there are robust reasons why the Church does not seek to
compete on exactly the same terms in this brave new world. However, as
the Church, we must be careful not to rely on others for information
about what we provide and surely the Church must be in the business of
promoting Christian marriage in a proactive way. This is an area where
we already have a Gospel mandate, to be 'wise as serpents' and 'innocent
as doves' (Matthew 10.16). So opening up the practice of marriage to
this whole wider context is a mission imperative for us as we begin the
twenty-first century.

Searching for companionship and commitment today

If weddings are taking place in a new environment, then marriage itself
is being lived out in a new context. Fewer people are getting married in
the UK and fewer of these marriages are taking place in church. Marriage
is lived out today in an atmosphere of lack of confidence in and growing

instability of long-term relationships. Society is becoming more individualistic, more mobile, less communal, less rooted. Recently, somebody was talking to me about their 'database community' in exactly the same terms I would use to describe our worshipping community. They were referring to a list of names and addresses on a computer, which functions as a means of distributing business information. But the way they talked about this community suggested the contacts knew each other, lived nearby each other and had some kind of affiliation. This community is not real but virtual, connected only by a microchip processor, not by a commitment to a common cause or activity demanding corporate behaviour. And yet this person spoke as if this electronic information had an identity and a reality of its own.

Nevertheless, despite the contemporary love affair with the virtual, the desire for companionship is as high as ever. The notion of finding one person with whom to share one's whole life is still held up as an ideal and yet is generally recognized as more difficult to attain than ever. Meeting on the Internet has become a recognized route for starting relationships, so that many people begin their search for their greatest single commitment with the click of a mouse, with all its remoteness. We live increasingly separate and remote lives, and use these individualistic ways to find companionship. The aspiration may be to find a permanent, fruitful relationship, but the *expectation* is often much less than that.

Commitment is therefore recognized as more than just contact and relationship. Commitment has a spiritual aspect and marriage is possibly just the highest form of that commitment rather than the recognized norm. Commitment is most commonly identified today by entering the housing market together rather than exchanging vows. Here are just a couple of quotations from some recent research into attitudes to marriage (see Chapter 3 for a more detailed discussion of recent findings):

> 'You can't get married and buy a house at the same time, it's far too expensive.'

> 'We'll get round to it some day . . . he keeps saying we'll get married once we've had the extension done.'[2]

It is over ten years since I took a wedding where the couple were not yet actually living together. Commitment is practical and emotional but that is still a long way from the mega commitment of marriage. One couple in our congregation have two children, jobs, a house, and recently have been dealing with the challenge of school admissions. We celebrate their wedding in four months' time, as they only now feel ready for that final piece of the jigsaw.

There are further barriers that hold couples back from the marriage commitment. There is a commonly held view that marriage is little different from cohabitation. This is, of course, confirmed by recent legislation and fiscal changes. As the argument goes: If a relationship is working, why change it? Why is it required that a public expression of this commitment is made, let alone a religious one?

The new commercial approach to weddings also holds people back, as couples see a wedding as a major financial outlay to be afforded at some time when enough of the mortgage has been paid. However, the desire to get married when it is time to start a family is still a strong one and many see this possibility as the time to formalize a commitment. One couple sitting in my study were quite happily talking about the fact that their whole wedding experience was going to cost them in excess of £30,000, as one last great splash before 'settling down' (and I was apologizing for the cost of the choir!). Also, these days I seem to be baptizing a lot of children soon after (or even just before) marrying their parents. Couples are marrying later in life (at the time of writing the average age for men is 31 and for women 29) and later in the life of their relationships, and this moment to formalize the pre-existent commitment (in all its forms) may be the 'default' decision moment for couples in the future. It's time to 'settle down' may still be the phrase on the lips of couples even in this mobile and virtual world.

As weddings themselves become grander and more elaborate, further possible conflicts arise. The wedding event becomes more of a barrier to marriage, not just in financial terms, but in social terms also. In our celebrity-wedding, style-aware culture, expectations of the quality of the event are higher than ever. Avoiding family politics may also lead to people procrastinating over the 'perfect day'. And, of course, as divorce becomes more prevalent and more people experience it in their families, couples become more fearful of making the same commitment only to have to go through the same messy process themselves some time in the future.

For all this, church weddings are often still seen as the real thing or the most traditional way of expressing a new marriage. The church 'white' wedding is still a widely received iconic image of what a wedding should be. If there is still something special and distinctive about the way people perceive getting married in church, then perhaps there is also a greater hesitation to choose this route if one is not 'religious' or a person of some faith already. Feeling hypocritical about marrying in church can be as much an excuse as an honourable position to avoid hypocrisy. Few couples understand that, under English Law, they have the right to be married in certain churches. There are those that think the traditional church wedding costs more than other forms of ceremony, just because it still has this aura of doing things properly. These are just some of the contemporary factors affecting marriage and weddings and the Church needs a response.

The church and weddings today

'Do you live in the parish?' How many times have you asked that question? How many times has that been the first response to an enquiry about getting married in church? In today's context, if our first response is one of qualification followed by the challenges of the diary, then we are not exactly giving ourselves the chance even to start with couples let alone accompany them on this most important of journeys. In my last year in a parish of 8,000 souls I conducted one wedding, and that was for members of the congregation. At no point did the parochial church council see it as the church's role to promote weddings or actively to go out and encourage people to be married in church. And when couples did come, how much was this a celebration with the worshipping community rather than just hiring a venue and a priest? We need to regain our self-confidence in weddings and see them for the mission opportunity that they are, as well as such a significant moment in the lives of two people as they become 'one flesh'. So while many fine clergy get this just right, in today's marriage climate, we can all look again at our ways of working with couples.

First, this requires a change of mindset, a regaining of belief in what church weddings have to offer. We need to remind ourselves that there is a proper and distinct place in contemporary society for church weddings. Perhaps Church schools offer a useful analogy. They compete educationally with other schools and should aim to offer the highest possible quality of education but, in addition, Church schools should be distinctive by their Christian ethos and character. Similarly, in the contemporary wedding market-place, church weddings ought to be both high-quality events and distinctive in ethos and character. They should be welcoming, moving, holy (spiritual) and memorable. It is clear that there is a place for church weddings if we recognize afresh and celebrate the distinctive qualities and values offered.

Secondly, we need to achieve clear, consistent and confident communication about what the Church stands for in marriage and, in particular, the celebration of weddings. Alongside the distinctive qualities mentioned above, ultimately what is on offer is a profound commitment between two persons who love one another, made in the presence of God, who is love. Of course, we *also* offer wonderful buildings that have a spiritual resonance and the time and commitment of professionals, who can become a soul friend, skilled in advising on marriage and the celebration of weddings.

Thirdly, we need to make clear and explicit the qualifications for marriage in church and communicate to all that the Church is delighted that couples want to be married in church. The new legislation regarding marriage qualification is designed to help with this vital ministry of welcome and insight. Even the language can still hinder us though. 'Qualification' is really a technical term that has 'pass or fail' overtones for a couple. You are in or you are out. Perhaps our language needs to change. Instead of qualification, perhaps when talking to couples we should speak of their 'special connection' to a church.

Fourthly, we need to be able to tailor weddings to the need and aspirations of couples so that the whole wedding experience becomes one of wonder and enjoyment and the service itself is clearly found to be the best part of their day.

And lastly, with these principles in place, we can be certain that weddings maintain their special place among the occasional offices and require our dedication and proclamation. We can be confident, for weddings *are* our business.

2

The measure of marriage

By the time you read this, the news will be out there and calls will be coming in. Couples will have heard that new laws apply to marriage qualification in England. The Church needs to be able to offer clear advice and teaching from the outset. This chapter discusses and suggests what sort of mindset we need in order to minister effectively in this new context.

It also provides some background and insight into the process leading to the new Marriage Measure (the full text of the Measure can be found in Appendix 1 on pp.119–25). So now for a *health warning:* reading about the decision-making processes of the General Synod may not be the most riveting thing you'll do today, so feel free to skip those sections. However, it is vital that we all understand how the Church has come to such a new position so that we can advise couples with confidence. When asked by members of the congregation 'Why has the Church done this?', we all need to know both the *why* and the *how*. It's also good to know that those who lead us take such care and attention over important changes.

After all that, there is an overview of how to respond to enquiries, together with answers to some of the most familiar questions.

The church that likes to say yes

Coming to work in the busiest parish church cathedral in England back in 2001 was daunting enough, let alone the prospect of having to take over and unravel the myriad qualification procedures for baptisms, weddings and funerals. Cathedrals are not bound by the usual parochial qualification routes for these services and even if the cathedral chapter chooses to work the normal parochial system, there are always exceptions to the rule, by the very nature of cathedral ministry. So it was invaluable to be given a run-down by one of my colleagues about how our cathedral dealt with such things. Just one side of A4 summarized the way qualifications for baptisms, weddings and funerals were determined, with particular reference to respecting the rights and responsibilities of the parishes around the cathedral. However, the most important advice was just one line and could be encapsulated in one word – YES. That was, and remains today, our starting position for enquiries for baptisms, weddings and funerals. This clear and positive mindset enables a number of different people within the organization to be able to respond with confidence to each enquiry. Not that every enquiry gets the go-ahead, but our philosophy is to give a clear indication of enthusiasm and pleasure at receiving such a request for ministry. Whatever their technical and legal status, above all, the enquirer should feel valued and taken seriously. After all, the telephone call or first approach is really important to them; this life event is probably the most pressing thing on their mind at that time. So whatever the individual church's response, it matters equally how that information is delivered. If the answer turns out to be a no, then it is the manner of communicating that news and the accompanying good advice that really matters. Expressions of condolence and congratulation are always valued, too, by people who come to us – whatever their circumstances.

All this is to underline the point that, while acknowledging that all legal requirements for marriage in church in England must continue to be fulfilled, when it comes to requests for marriage in church, our underlying mission and pastoral mindset must always be resoundingly positive.

Marriage legislation in England

The rules for qualification for marriage in England have served the Church well since the introduction of The Marriage Act 1949. These rules were established out of a sense of fairness and commitment to place, such as one's local church. They have also, effectively, provided an opportunity to draw people into greater commitment to their parish church or, beyond that, to deepen their understanding of the faith. Getting married in church can certainly be a moment that God uses to call people, at all levels of faith understanding, into a deeper relationship with him as well as with their chosen partner. It is important at this stage to stress that the law relating to marriage in church in England is not repealed at the advent of the new Marriage Measure. The previous legislation remains in force and can still be used as the most direct and obvious route to qualification. In brief, this long-lasting legislation is as follows:

- a person living in a parish may be married in their parish church following the publication of banns;

- a regular worshipper, on the electoral roll of the parish, may be married in their church, whether or not they live in the parish;

- a person who is unable to satisfy the residence or membership qualifications but who has a real and obvious connection with a particular parish may apply for a discretionary Archbishop's Special Licence.

This information is a summary only and does not include greater detail, for example, around whether a person has been previously married.

Now, the rules around marriage qualification have been interpreted and applied in a variety of ways down the years. Some clergy will see an opportunity for growth when couples attend a parish church in order to get on to the church's electoral roll. Others would want to avoid the electoral roll being used in this way if, once married, the couple no longer attend regularly. Similarly, couples have been known to stretch the facts of their residence details, especially where a parental address can be provided. Many of us actually leave home long before we see ourselves as having formally, finally moved out, but are we really still resident at home? But most people on all sides simply want to be honest and open about qualification. The clergy want to be pastoral and fulfil their legal responsibilities and sincere couples want to know the right thing to do and to feel wanted by the church they approach. So the clergy have the difficult task of balancing the requirements of state law with a pastoral concern for those who want God to be involved in their marriage. While some couples may be governed solely by venue, most seeking marriage in church have a desire somewhere within them, however they may articulate it, to be married in the 'sight of God'.

Over the years, couples have tended to be easily confused by these criteria or have found it difficult to understand why, at what is their happiest time, it appears that the Church does not want them. Clergy are well used to having to explain the complexities of qualification over and over again. Currently, I administer about 25 weddings a year, but it must be around 100 times a year that I have to explain why it is that couples can't immediately qualify for a marriage at St Albans Cathedral. This has to be done sensitively and with pastoral care but it doesn't always feel as if the conversation is successful. Such conversations often occur at an inopportune time, such as at the end of a service or on the telephone just before an appointment. In general, these legal qualifications have become cumbersome in today's highly mobile society and lack an understanding of the needs and circumstances of today's couples.

Changing the rules

So, if the legal constraints were beginning to creak and distract, it was time for the Church to grasp the nettle of reform. Before going into more detail about the Marriage Measure it will be helpful to canter briefly through some very recent Synod history and to take a look at the discussions, trials and tribulations involved in bringing about legislative change.

The workings of the General Synod may seem far removed from each and every wedding but the decision-making process of the Church at its highest levels does impact on real people in real parishes. It is important that clergy and parochial church councils own these decisions and understand why and how the Church has come to a new position. We are all local representatives of a greater whole. Understanding why the Church has changed the law of the land is just as important as knowing what the law is: we communicate this knowledge in advice we give to couples. A private member's motion on the subject of marriage legislation was first brought to the General Synod in 1996, requesting a new alternative to marriage by banns. Subsequent reports were published: *Just Cause or Impediment?* (2001) and *The Challenge to Change* (2002). In July 2002 the General Synod asked for work to begin on a new system of qualification entitled 'demonstrable connection'. Two years later a report, the *Marriage Law Review: Report by the Marriage Law Working Group* (GS 1543), was presented by the Bishop of Newcastle (The Rt Revd Martin Wharton). 'Demonstrable connection' was essentially defined as a wide-ranging list of family or historic connections with a parish church that could lead to qualification. The bishop hoped to test the mind of Synod in order to know how to progress further. The list of connections had been set to provide a generous but hopefully clear set of qualifications. The aim was that clergy would be able to change the way in which they worked with couples, especially at the point of first contact. So instead of having to say negatively, 'I am sorry, you cannot be married here because you do not live in this parish', clergy could sound more positive by saying, 'We would love you to marry here as long as you can demonstrate a connection to this particular parish or its church.' The proposed 'demonstrable connections' included attending the Church school, a uniformed youth organization or having had a grandparent worship in the church.

The General Synod enjoys flexing its muscles when it is asked for its mind to be tested, and in particular, enjoys discovering what its mind actually is through the cut and thrust of debate. Several speakers welcomed the new flexibility over the older legislation, particularly as it seemed in greater accord with the mission-shaped agenda so warmly welcomed at the previous meeting of Synod earlier that same year. However, Synod members were also concerned that the demonstrable connections were far too complicated and confusing. One speaker had worked out that this proposed legislation meant that he could probably be married in any one of the following places: Southend, Birmingham, Brighton and Hove, an Oxfordshire village, Liverpool, Tewkesbury, a number of parishes in London and the church of his confirmation, which was not his parish church at that time. He no longer had any personal connection with any of these places, and there could be still more places, as he was not certain where any of his grandparents had lived in the early part of their lives. He added that he had no current plans to marry not having yet found a suitable partner. No doubt when he did find the woman of his dreams, her demonstrable connections would add to the list in due course!

There were other amendments; specifically to open up marriage qualification completely. This would be similar to the European model where marriage takes place firstly in a civil ceremony and then moves on to church if a religious service is desired. Another proposal was to move to a celebrant-based system where ministers could perform weddings away from parish churches and authorized places of worship. The bishop had asked for a clear steer from Synod. In the end, he described the debate as a 'virtual dead heat' between those wanting some de-regulation and those wanting total de-regulation. Clearly, greater flexibility was required by the Church, but exactly how far that went and with what implications was now the question.

In July 2006 the then Dean of Wakefield, George Nairn-Briggs, brought the Draft Church of England Marriage Measure (GS 1616) to the General Synod for first consideration. In this draft, 'demonstrable connection' had become 'qualifying connection'. In his opening speech Nairn-Briggs asked the Synod to send this draft on to the revision stage, acknowledging that there would be alterations still to come. Throughout the debate there was still a concern that the connections had been drawn too widely. One speaker noted that his daughter already had enough connections to be married in any one of 50 parish churches, and this was just unworkable. Others were concerned about the practical implications of the draft proposals. Might such a wide range actually be undeliverable in terms of the man and woman power – volunteers, bell-ringers, organists and so on – required in churches that suddenly became available for a vastly increased number of weddings? Each and every practical concern was balanced by an equal and opposite desire to reach out in mission to couples as far as possible. So there was a call to be as welcoming as possible, as the draft legislation intended, but also a counter-balancing call for simplicity and clarity. Connections should not be so varied and complicated that couples might feel even more confused. Cathedrals were to be excluded from the legislation because the numbers of people who could claim a connection with a cathedral, under this legislation, were deemed to be too great and might have an adverse impact on the cathedrals' other main responsibilities. I believe that this aspect of the draft sowed a seed in the thoughts of Synod members that grew later into a realization that qualifying connection, however desirable in terms of the welcome it promised to provide, also needed to be deliverable for most parish churches in order for that promise to be achievable.

In February 2007 the matter returned as part of the revision process. In reality, the mind of Synod had moved since the previous summer and members had come to a clearer and tighter understanding of what a 'qualifying connection' constituted. Clearly, the people in the parishes had been giving this matter more serious consideration. However, in the process, in order to cope with all the various possibilities and confusions that might arise, the wide-ranging connections had become so redefined that *definitions* of the connections had taken over from the connections themselves. This was a far cry from the Synod's aim of opening up marriage qualification for mission purposes. The revision process had done its job according to the synodical process, but this had not allowed for new creativity to flow from years of debate and consideration. The Bishop of Willesden (The Rt Revd Pete Broadbent) summed up the concern in his inimitable style. The draft revision was described as a pile of regulations that were completely inoperable and 'a load of old codswallop'. Another area that raised issues was that of worship and 'habitual attendance'. Most parochial clergy had managed to work with this requirement for many years, even making it a mission opportunity. However, in order to define this in legal terms for the new legislation, Synod was advised that habitual attendance really meant attending church three times a year, over a period of six months, although, in law, it could be argued that going to church just once constituted habitual attendance. The new law was well on the way to becoming the proverbial ass. There were pleas for simplicity and manageability. Motions to 'take note' are rarely refused and so the motion was carried in order to move on to the more detailed revision stage. It is surprising how the mood of Synod can be a tangible force for change.

In the summer of 2007, at the July Synod in York, the Church had two bites at the cherry of legislative change and we moved into a different gear. On the second day of meeting, the report of the Revision Committee was made, with Synod time allocated (if the debate went well) for final approval on the last day of the Synod. Things were at last moving at speed. The media had taken remarkable interest in this internal wrangling and clergy were already receiving telephone calls from couples about 2009 weddings that might come under any new legislation. The revised text moved successfully on to its final stage. So in the last session of the Synod meeting everybody knew what was at stake. There was a chance to send draft legislation to Parliament that would radically change weddings in England for the first time in over 60 years. When sending legislation to Parliament, the final debate in Synod is different in that anyone who wishes to must be allowed to speak, so that everyone has been heard. It is a fine Anglican tradition.

The patient Dean of Wakefield reminded Synod that the legislation regarding marriage had been formulated not by the Church but by the State in 1949. Here was the chance for the Church to speak about getting married in church and God's love, represented especially by our welcome. He stated that this was a much more pastoral approach, establishing the principle of 'connection' over against simply that of residence. Again the Synod was also reminded that any new legislation added to the 1949 Act of Parliament but did not repeal it. The new list of connections, as amended by the synodical process, was described as simple and user-friendly, to be supplemented by new guidance and resource material. The dean highlighted that in working through this long process of drafting legislation, the Church had emphasized the importance of the institution of marriage in welcoming and encouraging couples who come to the church at the most significant time of their lives. The Revd Jan McFarlane from Norwich supported the motion with this comment:

> So anything that allows us to offer such couples the warmest and the most accommodating welcome is surely to be encouraged. Please, let us approve this Measure with wholehearted enthusiasm and make the passing of it a new chapter in our outreach to those who are hovering nervously on the very edges of our Church, just waiting to be welcomed in.[3]

The voting was by Houses to give as clear a picture as possible of support from within the Church to Parliament. Support was resounding.

	Ayes	Noes
House of Bishops	26	0
House of Clergy	106	3
House of Laity	123	3

The Marriage Measure went before the Ecclesiastical Committee of Parliament on 22 April 2008. There was considerable media interest in the changes. BBC Radio 5 Live gave over 30 minutes to discussing the issues involved and there were several newspaper articles the following day with headlines such as 'Anglican leaders vow to relax rules for traditional white wedding – in a church of couple's choice'. It is not often that the media take such interest in a law that has yet to be seen by either the House of Commons or the House of Lords, let alone to become the law of the land, especially when it is initiated by the Church.

The new Marriage Measure 2008

Here is another, more user-friendly summary of the new qualifications for marriage in the Church of England, addressed to couples for ease of description.

You will be able to be married in your parish church of choice if you can demonstrate just one of the following 'qualifying connections'.

That:

- One of you was baptized in the parish concerned.

- One of you has been confirmed, and was prepared for confirmation in the parish.

- One of you has at any time lived in the parish for at least six months.

- One of you has habitually attended public worship in the parish for at least six months (which means attending at least three times a year – e.g. at Christmas, Easter and Pentecost – over a period of years or more regularly over a shorter period).

Or:

- One of you has a parent who has lived in the parish for at least six months any time after you were born (or, in the case of your fiancé/e's parents, any time after your fiancé/e was born).

- One of you has a parent who has regularly been to normal services in the parish church for at least six months any time after you (or your fiancé/e) were born.

- Either of you has a parent or grandparent who was married in the parish.

In all cases – i.e. going to normal services, baptism, confirmation or marriage – this applies only to Church of England services. Even if you cannot demonstrate any of the above connections, we want to help you explore whether it may still be possible for you to marry in your special church. Talk to the priest there well in advance to discuss the options open to you.

Any such summary raises questions about further information, such as access to clergy, date and time of a wedding service in church, and marriages for those previously married, but these matters are best dealt with once a personal contact and relationship has been established with the priest.

Guidance for clergy and parishes

When enquiries regarding the Measure started to come in, the Church of England provided some initial guidance for clergy, parishes and couples. Here is an adapted summary answering several commonly asked questions.

Why has the Church changed the rules regarding marriage qualification?

When a couple decide to come to the Church for marriage and to enter into a lifelong commitment to one another before God, they may wish to do so in a place where neither of them is living or on the electoral roll, but which has particular and enduring significance for one or both of them. For example, in a substantial number of cases, the couple wish to marry in the place where one of them grew up and/or where his or her parents now live, and which he or she sees as home even though he or she is not resident there as a matter of law. The Church recognizes this, and wishes the parish to be in the position of offering such a couple the same welcome as it does to those living in the parish. This means the need for an Archbishop's Special Licence will no longer be necessary in a large number of cases.

Is it possible to have a Church of England service in places other than in a parish church?

Yes. Under existing law, the marriage can take place in cathedrals, schools or college chapels but they are not covered by the 2008 Measure and the Archbishop's Special Licence is usually required.

What evidence will need to be produced in order to prove a 'qualifying connection'?

It will be necessary to provide the information, written or otherwise, that the minister of the parish where a couple hopes to marry requires in order to satisfy himself or herself that one of you has a 'qualifying connection'. The House of Bishops have issued full advice available at http://www.yourchurchwedding.org/default.aspx

A couple wish to be married in a church with which they feel they have a link but not a qualifying connection under the Measure. What is the way forward for them?

The two ways in which it may be possible for a couple to put themselves in a position to be able to marry in the parish in question, under the existing law, are:

- for one or both of the couple to attend public worship in the parish habitually for at least six months and apply for entry on the church electoral roll; or

- to apply for a Special Licence, with the consent of the minister in charge of the church where the couple wish to marry. (The grant of a Special Licence is always discretionary, but favourable consideration is likely to be given to the application where a couple can show a connection with the parish. Further information, including details of the normal requirements, can be obtained from Faculty Office of the Archbishop of Canterbury at 1 The Sanctuary, London SW1P 3JT, telephone 020 7222 5381, or from the Faculty Office web site at www.facultyoffice.org.uk)

The new Measure does not affect the law on either of these alternatives.

Couples should be advised to discuss the position as soon as possible with the parish priest of the parish in question (or a person authorized to deal with such enquires on his or her behalf).

Where do banns need to be read under the 'qualifying connection route'?

Banns must be read in the parish or parishes where each member of the couple is resident, and in the parish where the marriage is to take place.

One member of the couple is divorced and wanting to marry for the second time. Does this make a difference under the new Measure?

A parish priest, whether of a home parish or a parish where a couple have a 'qualifying connection', is not under a legal duty to marry if the divorced person's former spouse is still alive. The bishops have issued Advice for Clergy on these cases, and that advice and further information, including a leaflet with an application form for couples, is available at: http://www.cofe.anglican.org/info/papers/mcad/index.html

If a common licence has to be used (for example, if one member of the couple has been temporarily abroad and so could not have banns read), how does this work in relation to the Measure?

The Measure makes it possible to issue a common licence for a marriage in the parish church of a parish with which one or both of the couple have a 'qualifying connection', subject to special provisions as to the procedure. Couples should be advised to discuss this with the parish priest of the parish where they wish to be married.

If one or both of the couple are not members of the Church of England/or are not baptized/or are not Christians, will this make any difference to whether the new Measure can be used?

No, provided the couple both understand and accept that a member of the Church of England clergy would have to take the marriage service and would have to use a legally authorized form of Church of England marriage service.

What of marriage preparation under this Measure, especially if the couple live a considerable distance from the church in which they wish to be married?

There are two separate aspects to marriage preparation.

The first is that, before any couple are married, the minister of the church where they are to be married is under an obligation to talk to them both about the commitment they are proposing to enter into. Proper and practical arrangements for this engagement for all involved will need to be made in the preparation for a service.

In addition, Church of England parishes in general offer couples a good deal more than the legal minimum by way of marriage preparation, such as a course of sessions, sometimes with other couples. Most couples appreciate taking part in these and find them very valuable, because they help couples to lay a solid foundation for their life together. For example, the course often offers couples an opportunity to talk through some of the important issues, hopes and fears that will form a vital part of their future married life. If the couple are too far away from the parish where they hope to be married to be able to take advantage of the marriage preparation arranged in that parish, it may well be possible to arrange for them to go to sessions in a parish near their home, and this is something that they should discuss at an early stage with the minister of the parish where they hope to marry. The Church has the opportunity and responsibility here to ensure marriage preparation takes place and help the couple feel rooted in the place and parish where they live. This broadens marriage preparation into a further mission opportunity.

3

Marriage: research and reality
Lynda Barley

Many clergy don't rate research and statistics. It is not that clergy refute such information but rather that the bare bones of data do not tell a life story, or speak of the small ways in which each and every pastoral encounter is unique. However, the research findings discussed here are of great encouragement and help to us all.

The Revd Lynda Barley is the Head of Research and Statistics at the Archbishops' Council and has a track record in providing clear and strategic information for all aspects of mission and ministry today. Her approach is accessible and grounded in reality. Focusing on what real couples have to say, the research she outlines in what follows supports the impetus for legislative change and the need for a new awareness of the needs and aspirations of couples today.

Modern-day marriages

It seems that all the statistics point towards the fact that marriage is out of fashion. But is it really? A closer look beyond the news headlines reveals a Britain where most people are still married. There is evidence to show that couples today delay getting married but marriage is not being deserted in droves. Many couples live together before they marry, they have more choice about where and when they marry, but they still marry. It is easy to look at modern-day marriage statistics and conclude that we value marriage less perhaps because we live more independently than in the past. But recent research into marriage challenges this, concluding with an altogether different perspective:[4]

> 'In the past, people had to marry – but today, people want to . . . although marriage is out of reach for many.'

What is it that in modern Britain draws couples to marriage as a way of life and to their own wedding day? And why is it out of reach for many couples? Does the Church have a pastoral ministry to modern-day couples wanting to get married? The Archbishops' Council identified the issue and invested in extensive research with an eminent and widely respected research company, Henley Centre Headlight Vision. In 2007 they carried out research across Britain to discover more about modern-day marriages and this chapter shares some of the surprises we discovered and reflects briefly on some pastoral responses.

An aspiration for life

Marriage for life remains an aspiration for many couples. In our national research 38 per cent of unmarried women and almost the same proportion, 36 per cent, of unmarried men aspired to marriage. Marriage remains 'the ultimate commitment' for many. Yes, it 'ties the knot' but for most people it signals rather than generates commitment. Men and women commented that marriage is 'the final piece of the jigsaw' and 'the final frontier'. It is not always the defining moment in a relationship. That might be seen to be a practical sign of commitment such as living together or opening a shared bank account. It could also be the unspoken realization: 'you just know that is the person you hope to spend the rest of your life with'. But marriage signifies a *completing* of a committed relationship: 'I want you to be my husband, not just the bloke I live with', said one woman to her partner. We found 42 per cent of adults think that marriage is the event that *most* indicates that people have entered a serious relationship, compared to 21 per cent, who believe that moving in together and 18 per cent, who believe that having children together, mark the point of commitment. Men, in particular, think long and carefully about the commitment of marriage. Contrary to popular opinion their attitude is far from casual. One man commented:

> 'Marriage is definitely a big commitment . . . preparation classes at church might put some people off but that could be a good thing.'

For many couples, the desire to start a family is the key trigger to make the marriage commitment. Marriage is for them a natural progression in their relationship and good for them and for society. A staggering 86 per cent of married people and 64 per cent of unmarried people are mindful of the challenge of the marriage commitment but agree that it is important for society. Even with the high incidence of marriage breakdown today, marriage is taken very seriously. We were amazed to discover that 85 per cent of married people and 59 per cent of unmarried people believe it is the most serious decision of life. Separate research confirms these findings and reveals that 7 in 10 young adults and 8 in 10 of those who are cohabiting want to wed.[5] The most frequent reasons given were to indicate commitment and to provide a stable environment to bring up children.

So the goal posts have moved. Marriage is viewed differently but marriage is still greatly valued by the majority of the population.

Bride or groom?

When we interviewed couples in our research, one of the main findings was a growing disconnectedness between the marriage ceremony and the marriage itself. This plays itself out, broadly speaking, in the differences between the attitudes and experiences of women and of men. When sidespeople ask 'bride or groom's side?' they could be highlighting more of a difference than they realize. Couples agree that the primary reason to have a wedding is to get married to the person you love but beyond that men and women view the wedding day very differently. Both accept that part of the reason for having a wedding is to indulge their partner's wedding dreams. As they plan the day together couples may find it to be 'a real bonding experience' (as one man put it), but frequently the bride becomes the centre of attention and grooms let their partner make most of the decisions about the wedding day itself.

Yet to portray grooms as somewhat indifferent and uncommitted would be a shallow interpretation. They were more focused in our discussions than their fiancées on the serious aspect to the event. Several men in our research were keen on the idea of marriage preparation sessions to check they were doing the right thing by getting married. One man put it this way: 'Marriage is for life but a wedding is a glorified party.' In planning their wedding, men were frequently more focused on the commitment of marriage while women were often more focused on the wedding day and making it perfect for the couple, their families and friends.

We discovered that although men and women view weddings differently, they are both committed to marriage but they don't realize this about each other! We were surprised to hear couples being quite cynical about the other's motivations for marriage. Overall, 21 per cent of women think most men get married because of family pressure although only 12 per cent of men believe this to be the case. Men, in turn, equally believe that women get married in order to start a family or to have a family. Both sexes think their partner is less likely to want to marry in order to feel more committed than is, in fact, the case. Brides and grooms find it difficult to discuss their marriage commitment apart from all the trappings of the wedding day and it is the grooms that appear most conscious of this. Men are more likely than women to see marriage as a sign of commitment, while women are more likely to see it as completing their relationship. Men may appear to be commitment-phobic but this is because even though divorce is much easier today, in reality, they take marriage very seriously and would like the opportunity to discuss it with the assistance of an independent professional. The research shows that couples value support before (and even after) their wedding day but brides and grooms need different and yet complementary approaches, perhaps providing the opportunity for them to understand each other better.

The perfect day

Modern-day couples can choose to get married almost anywhere by any authorized registrar. So what attracts couples to get married in church and what puts them off?

Weddings are often promoted as 'the best day of your life'. In fact, in our research, 71 per cent of married people said their wedding was the most important day of their life. So couples want to make their wedding day as memorable as possible, often highly personalized. We live in a consumer culture and it is the ethos of that culture that has taken over the wedding day. There are numerous industries that depend on the wedding market and recent changes in marriage legislation offer the opportunity for once-in-a-lifetime experiences of all sorts. There appears to be no limit to the imaginative ways couples make their vows to each other on their wedding day, from underwater diving to parachuting to quiet moments on a beach. There is considerable demand, for example, for the wedding package being offered by the London Eye where the ceremony is conducted high above the London skyline while the guests enjoy the view in accompanying pods. Eleven per cent of British couples now get married abroad, which means that churches, for example, are seen as just one possible venue in a wide spectrum of options. If couples do not like the wedding day experience on offer at their local church they will (and do) go elsewhere, often somewhere with no religious link. We found that sometimes couples want a church wedding but what they perceive as unnecessary rules send them to more 'open-minded' venues.

Making a wedding day as perfect as possible means providing a highly individualized approach, which can present challenges to any institution. But then institutions are not very popular today. Couples in our research often rejected the idea that their relationship needed to be affirmed by an external institution. Here is the tension between the private and the public aspects to getting married. Many couples today do not see the need for the formal public affirmation that marriage brings. Their relationship is private and often no less committed for that. They frequently have little experience of church worship and shy away from formal church. Public displays of affirmation do not attract everyone as one man's view shows:

> 'I just don't see what the point of marriage is . . . Marriage is a dying breed, it will die out eventually and people will just live together.'

The rising tide of individualism encourages couples to cement relationships their way, which may or may not involve marriage and a wedding.

Amidst this consumer culture, the Church has one asset up its sleeve that can cut across all the rules and rituals in the eyes of many couples – the vicar! The person conducting a wedding can make the ceremony highly personal. Couples, in our research, largely spoke about the vicar extremely warmly although often they had not expected this to be the case. They used words like 'modern', 'not too stiff' and 'appropriate but not too matey'. The wedding can be 'more personal' if they are able to build up a relationship with the vicar who is marrying them. Couples enormously appreciated this and felt that it can 'make the day'. One groom remarked: 'You don't get the feeling of being on a treadmill in church', while a bride commented: 'The ceremony was really warm and personal; he (the vicar) wasn't just reading from a book.'

Parish clergy can be the key that unlocks a unique personalized wedding service. They can make or break the perfect day – they can create a unique beginning to the institution of marriage.

A proper wedding

Couples want their perfect wedding day, but what makes them feel that they have been 'properly' married?

For better or worse, everyone brings their expectations to a wedding and couples can feel it impossible to please parents, friends and themselves in equal measure. Such is the pressure to organize the memorable event that the wedding can even be delayed or put off. Managing the politics of an extended family on the wedding day can in itself be a headache for the bride and groom. Added to that can be the expectation of relatives for a 'proper' wedding. Couples save until they can afford to marry properly. One couple we spoke to wanted to get the extension done at home first: 'You can't get married and buy a house at the same time, it's far too expensive.'

For most couples the idea of a budget wedding is entirely unacceptable, so they live together until they can afford the wedding of their dreams. They may have children and, as there are few time pressures to get married, they wait until they can afford the wedding they desire and can do it properly both for themselves and their families. Sadly, it is the expense of a proper wedding today that can put it 'out of reach' for many couples.

But what do couples want in a proper wedding? For some it is connected with tradition and church can be part of this package. Only 23 per cent of adults feel that church weddings are too traditional but this remains a significant proportion. Couples can be attracted by the idea of a traditional white wedding with bells, old car, aisle and organ but they can find this a deterrent and aspire to an alternative, more personalized wedding. Traditional roots are important to some but a barrier to others who prefer modern-day relevance. Churches today are being challenged to build on their traditional roots and be culturally relevant in many aspects of church life. They cannot escape this challenge too in the wedding experience churches offer and, as the eligibility rules for church weddings are being relaxed, this challenge becomes more acute.

If couples are not necessarily looking for 'tradition' in a proper wedding, what are they seeking? Over half (53 per cent) of all adults consider a church wedding to be more 'proper' than one taking place elsewhere and, surprisingly, younger people and men were more likely to hold this view. Among those planning a church wedding we found that 75 per cent felt this was part of having a proper wedding but they found it hard to articulate the reasons for this linkage. For some 'the fairytale wedding' of their childhood involves a church, for others it's the solemn or even sacred atmosphere that adds more weight to the commitment. Even if 'God is not invited to the wedding', many couples chose a church wedding believing that a marriage commitment made in church is more weighty than one made in a non-religious venue. Thirty-eight per cent of adults agree with this sentiment. The Church is seen as one of the few credible voices in contemporary society that demonstrates that it takes commitment seriously and, for many, this is part of the attraction of having a church wedding. Sixty-six per cent of adults feel that the Church is an enthusiastic believer in marriage.[6] Fifty-three per cent believe that the gravitas of a commitment in the institution of the Church is a significant draw for a proper wedding:

> 'You're getting married in the eyes of God, which is a bit stronger.'

This is hugely encouraging for all those who engage in this vital area of the Church's ministry. For modern-day couples being 'properly' married is to be married in the sight of God supported by the prayers of friends, family and church.

Sacred space

How do people who want to get married in church relate to the spiritual aspect of what is going on? People in Britain today do not generally consider themselves to be religious, but they will readily admit to being spiritual. People still pray (between 2 in 5 and 3 in 5 in various recent surveys), but churchgoing is out of fashion. We know that 1 in 5 adults in our cities, towns and countryside drops by into a local church or chapel to find a quiet, sacred space.[7] Our churches should be open to the nation beyond Sundays, across the ordinary working week and on Saturdays. In our research we discovered just as much enthusiasm for churches to be open for weddings whatever day of the week. Many wedding couples feel that the solemn, even sacred atmosphere of church buildings adds more emotion and potentially more weight to the event. One groom wanted a quiet opportunity in the wedding service for him and his fiancée to reflect alone on what they had done. We are finding that he is typical of many. We found that it is not just regular churchgoers that want to be married 'in the eyes of God'. Belief in God is not solely associated with churchgoing:

> 'I work really long hours so my weekend is precious to me . . . church doesn't fit with my lifestyle . . . but it doesn't mean I don't have some religious beliefs.'

Couples take the religious views of their partner seriously too. Fifty-six per cent said that their own or their partner's religion was important in their decision to get married in church and not so many fewer, 47 per cent, said that their family's religious beliefs also had an influence.

But we must address the issue that religion is a barrier for some. In our research 57 per cent of couples not planning to marry in church said that not attending church regularly or not feeling religious enough was an important factor in their decision. These couples frequently said that they would feel hypocritical getting married in church. A number, in fact, find the idea quite appealing but have such respect for the institution that even if they have a belief in God they don't feel sufficiently religious to qualify. They believe that you need to be religious to have permission to get married in church and equate being religious with regular church attendance. Such couples are not aware that they have a right to be married in their local church and are more concerned about proving they are good enough for the Church. They may have a sentimental link with a particular church, but they worry about 'the grilling' they will receive when they first meet the vicar and are genuinely confused about who can get married in church. The vicar may be trying to be friendly and get to know the couple but for men, in particular, this first meeting is a daunting prospect: 'Meeting the vicar is like a job interview, like you have to sell yourself to him.'

Finding a vicar who couples want to perform the ceremony is important, and for 17 per cent of couples such problems caused them to go elsewhere. If couples do not feel welcome they often move on, not to another church, but to a venue that has no religious associations and an opportunity for contact with church at a pivotal point in their lives is lost.

A warm welcome and parish clergy are key to the decision to marry in church – particularly for men, who are less inclined to think that a church wedding is their right. But, if couples do decide to marry in church they can also be attracted by one surprise that many churches now provide. Marriage preparation sessions proved to be popular with a large number of couples, though it was a turn-off for some. Grooms, in particular, value the opportunity to discuss married life with a professional and such sessions individually or in a group are attractive to a significant number. Thirty-six per cent of couples getting married in church said the sessions offered by the church were an important part of their decision. A significant proportion, 44 per cent, were broadly in favour of the idea that the church should be supporting married life before the wedding day and 39 per cent of the general public said that churches should offer follow-up support after the wedding day.

This should encourage churches to maintain and develop contact. There are good opportunities to establish ongoing contact: invitations to church to hear their banns, after couples return from honeymoon, first anniversaries and many church festivals. Churches are discovering a warm response to wedding festivals and anniversary invitations to a special church service. Vicars, marriage preparation and sacred space can still add up to a strong church wedding package for today's wedding couples. Churches are more welcome in the lives of newly married couples than we appreciate. The Church in turn needs to take more seriously its welcome towards them. In an open Church, a church wedding can sow the seed for Christian marriage.

So, in summary, the Henley Centre Headlight Vision research provides important insights into the modern-day marriage market.

1. There is 'space' within contemporary society for the Church to talk positively about marriage.

2. There is a need for clear, coherent and unapologetic

communication about what the Church does, in fact, stand for in relation to marriage.

3. There is a need for the Church to make explicit the implicit understandings within the Church about who is entitled to a church wedding, and actively to reassure couples that the Church is happy to marry them.

4. Brides and grooms have different expectations of a church wedding experience, and it is important that clergy are aware of these and communications tailored accordingly where possible.

5. The unique personal dimension of a church wedding is a huge potential draw, which the Church should emphasize. Couples value the sacred and solemn aspects to church weddings.

6. Couples can be apprehensive in their first contact with the vicar and the church. The welcome they receive may decide whether they have a church wedding at all.

7. Couples value the vicar and are open to establishing further contact with their local church.

8. Couples preparing for marriage and planning a wedding have many anxieties in which they welcome the Church's interest. The Church could look to partially alleviate these and offer an after-care service.

4

Turning water into wine

On the third day there was a wedding in Cana of Galilee, and the mother of Jesus was there. Jesus and his disciples had also been invited to the wedding. When the wine gave out, the mother of Jesus said to him, 'They have no wine.' And Jesus said to her, 'Woman, what concern is that to you and to me? My hour has not yet come.' His mother said to the servants, 'Do whatever he tells you.' Now standing there were six stone water-jars for the Jewish rites of purification, each holding twenty or thirty gallons. Jesus said to them, 'Fill the jars with water.' And they filled them up to the brim. He said to them, 'Now draw some out, and take it to the chief steward.' So they took it. When the steward tasted the water that had become wine, and did not know where it came from (though the servants who had drawn the water knew), the steward called the bridegroom and said to him, 'Everyone serves the good wine first, and then the inferior wine after the guests have become drunk. But you have kept the good wine until now.' Jesus did this, the first of his signs, in Cana of Galilee, and revealed his glory; and his disciples believed in him.

(John 2.1-11)

Cana in Galilee

Pilgrims to the Holy Land invariably take in a visit to Cana in Galilee. Cana is a disappointment. Unlike many of the more popular sites there is little provision for visitors. Coaches have to pull up on the wrong side of the road and enthusiastic pilgrims have to dice with death in crossing the busy road from Galilee to Nazareth. The local drivers have no sympathy for ambulatory Anglicans. Then your guide takes you up what looks like a back street (that's because it *is* a back street) to reach a humble church within which you will find a number of stone jars. Debates as to the authenticity of these jars are pointless as they do roughly represent what would have been in use in the time of Jesus, and stone water jars were not exactly rare. Pilgrims hear the Gospel reading and some couples reaffirm their marriage vows, some pray for their absent spouse, some pray to get lucky and others just pray. It is a short visit with the inevitable stop on the way out at the Cana in Galilee Wine Store. The storekeeper takes great pride in selling you your essential bottle of Cana wine. Like the stone jars, it's not original, which is just as well. For if this was the wine Jesus provided at the wedding in John's Gospel, either the miracle left a bit to be desired or the chief steward had drunk too much of the other stuff already! It's not good but it is memorable. According to the storekeeper there are different grades of Cana wine and the best wine is quite special. I had some on my last visit to the Holy Land. Obviously the storekeeper is a descendant of the chief steward.

While 1 Corinthians 13 may be the most popular scriptural reading at weddings, John 2.1-11 comes a close second and ought to be encouraged. Reference is made to this vital passage both in the Pastoral Introduction and the Preface (to the *Common Worship* Marriage Service). The Preface says: 'Marriage is a way of life made holy by God, and blessed by the presence of our Lord Jesus Christ with those celebrating a wedding at Cana in Galilee.' The account of Jesus' first miracle is central to our understanding of Christian marriage and encapsulates the spiritual dimension so often felt but not articulated by couples. We share with Jesus in the task of turning water into wine, of turning man and woman into husband and wife, and the enquiring couple into the married faithful, and we should not assume that couples do not have the potential for taking on board the importance of Jesus' teaching. Indeed, perhaps it is this underlying hope that has brought them to enquire about marriage in church. When this Bible passage is opened to them rather than preached to them, couples are able to find that spiritual aspect they were hoping for when they decided to contact the vicar.

Understanding Cana

What is really going on here? How can this gospel story, which is familiar even to some of the un-churched, help couples see Jesus as the one who can transform lives and who acts in our own situations and life events?

We must always be careful not to read too much into a gospel account, or to emphasize one aspect of a multi-layered event to the detriment of its overall message, but it is possible here for couples to see at least something of the spiritual dimension of their love for each other, in Christ. So, what follows is more of a reflection than a biblical exegesis, more of a sermon than a lecture. Ministers need to find their own way of telling the gospel stories so that they come alive and impact on those in their care. How can we communicate all this to couples seeking marriage? Here is just one example, the approach I most often use when describing how we see marriage through the eyes of Scripture.

What is really going on here fundamentally is that we are discovering good news about who Jesus is. At a very obvious level he is someone who affirms community and marriage itself. The setting of a wedding carries overtones of the biblical idea of God's covenant with his people. In this analogy the human relationship of faithful love and commitment between husband and wife is intertwined with the knowledge of God's faithful love and commitment to his people, so that each sheds light on the other. The New Testament takes up the Old Testament vision of the arrival of God's kingdom being like the joy of a marriage feast. Jesus speaks of himself as the bridegroom of Israel (Mark 2.18-20) and the imagery is taken up further in John 3.29f. The choice of this event of celebration for the first manifestation of Jesus' glory (2.11) not only testifies to him as the expression of God's love and the bringer of salvation, but highlights the relationship of marriage itself as a place where divine and spiritual realities are experienced. That in turn implies the importance of marriage for a healthy human society.

At another level we discover that Jesus has a unique gift to be able to change what we take for granted; that is, water into wine, lack into surplus and sadness into hope. Stone water jars contain water, everyday water, and they become filled with the best wine that will last and mature. Couples come together as individuals, and through their commitment to each other and God's blessing, they are changed into something new, something unique and more wonderful than before. By their coming together in love, fidelity and self-giving they imitate Christ in his ministry among us. The ordinary stuff of their lives, when offered to God in Christ, is rescued and completed and enhanced beyond their expectations. We might note Mary's words to the servants in 2.5: 'Do whatever he tells you.' Simple faith and obedience to the commands of Christ count for a lot in marriage, as elsewhere. Married couples soon realize that it is not the trimmings of the wedding that last, but their commitment in love for each other that makes a love worth keeping and sharing. At the marriage in Cana, we see water changed into wine but it is we who, in marriage, are changed by the love of God in Christ, and that really is something worth celebrating.

And at yet another level, we find that Jesus is the bridegroom at God's heavenly and glorious marriage feast. John's presentation of the story of Cana proclaims that while the Judaism of Jesus' day offered purification through washing with water, the purification and renewal of God's people would finally come only through Jesus' act of self-giving on the cross (referred to throughout the Gospel, as in 2.4, as his 'hour'). This link between washing and the action of Jesus in laying down his life is made powerfully and memorably in the foot-washing and teaching of John 13.1-17. There Jesus makes it clear that his self-giving is not only a unique act of salvation but an example for his disciples, leading to the new commandment, 'Love one another as I have loved you'. If the sacrificial surrender of the cross sums up the impact of Jesus on human life, it should be no surprise that when the Letter to the Ephesians (5.21-32) compares the relationship of husband and wife with that between Christ and the Church, it is that self-giving that is central. It defines the quality of love that husbands and wives are called and enabled by God to offer to each other. So the Alternative Preface to the service says, 'It is God's purpose that, as husband and wife give themselves to each other in love throughout their lives, they shall be united in that love as Christ is united with his Church.'[8] What we believe about Jesus influences what we believe about marriage and ultimately about each other.

Marriage is one of the sacramental acts of the Church. A sacrament is an outward and visible sign of an inward and spiritual gift. The outward and visible sign of marriage is the making of vows, the joining of hands and the exchange of rings. The inward and spiritual gift is the joining of souls and that gift is Jesus acting in the lives of couples today. In this next section I look at how marriage might be interpreted to the couple from this perspective.

The professional marriage minister

Marriage has often been described as a sacrament because it belongs to the class of symbolic actions through which the purposes of God for human beings are both expressed and enacted. In a world where so much is temporary and subjective, the sacramental life of the Church stands as a counter-cultural way of understanding the world and God's activity within it because it conveys God's promises and involves people in a response of faith and commitment, primarily in the rites of baptism and the Eucharist. Marriage stands apart from other sacramental acts in two respects. First, it is a sacrament that belongs to the created order, as it is the blessing of an institution intended by God for all human societies. Secondly, in marriage, it is the couple, through the joining of hands and the exchange of vows, who make the marriage happen. Only after these things does the Church act, as the priest seals and blesses the new relationship. This means that the task of the professional marriage minister is to enable the true ministers of the sacrament to understand what they are doing with all its deepest significance. (Every priest – stipendiary and otherwise – is a professional marriage minister by virtue of ordination.) We are not doing it for them or to them as with some of the other sacraments. The couple are 'priests to each other' and this means that they can engage with God's love and their love for each other in a wholly wonderful way and in an ever-deepening, developing, sacrificial relationship. So when a couple come to the Church for marriage, the task of the priest is to work with them, bringing professional expertise and experience, sharing theological insight and liturgical formation with the couple who will, on the day, bring all this together in each other. This is a unique responsibility and requires a greater degree of selflessness and sharing on the part of the priest than otherwise might be usual. Marriages are exclusive relationships, but for the purpose of preparation, planning and celebration, three's company and two is a crowd.

So what does the priest bring to this sacramental party? The first thing is, of course, a biblical perspective. The wedding at Cana summarizes a good deal of the Christian understanding for the celebration of marriage but there is much more. 'God is love and those who live in love live in God and God lives in them' (1 John 4.16b). If, as Christians, we believe that God is love then God is involved and wants to be involved in loving relationships. The Preface to the Marriage Service states 'Marriage is a gift of God in creation through which husband and wife may know the grace of God'. By being married, couples have the opportunity to know God more fully. We know God to be a God of relationship, and by committing themselves so fully to each other, couples can discover more about the God who is himself in relationship as Father, Son and Holy Spirit. From the beginning of the Old Testament, Scripture teaches us the value of marriage and the mess created when such commitment goes wrong. Jesus himself valued marriage, even though he himself was unmarried, and it is probably no mistake or coincidence that his first miracle took place at a wedding.

So, in marriage, the minister brings first and foremost this rich deposit of faith and revelation to give depth and articulation to the feelings expressed by a couple. The suggested wedding readings in *Common Worship* point this out and give us a wealth of poetry, psalmody, teaching, hope and encouragement for couples and clergy alike.

Beloved, let us love one another, because love is from God; everyone who loves is born of God and knows God. Whoever does not love does not know God, for God is love. God's love was revealed among us in this way: God sent his only Son into the world so that we might live through him. In this is love, not that we loved God but that he loved us and sent his Son to be the atoning sacrifice for our sins. Beloved, since God loved us so much, we also ought to love one another. No one has ever seen God; if we love one another, God lives in us, and his love is perfected in us.

(1 John 4.7-12)

The second professional contribution is the ministry of the Church. We believe that, as the Preface continues, 'as man and woman grow together in love and trust, they shall be united with one another in heart, body and mind, as Christ is united with his bride, the Church'. This unseen but tangible union between Christ and his Church is a good image for couples. The Church cannot function without Christ; without him we would be simply a human organization that would have failed long ago. Christ likewise can use the Church here on earth to extend his kingdom and to be an example to the rest of creation. In marriage, each person brings something unique but complementary and it is together that something greater than the sum of the parts is found, something holy. The Church can say to couples that God, who is the source of life and love, has already begun his work within them and that without him their marriage may well be less than it can be, that is, a spiritual union as well as a physical or emotional union. The Church can also say that entering marriage is the opportunity for a new beginning and that, before vows are exchanged, reflection and repentance can take place. The Church has the authority to challenge couples to be able to leave the past behind.

The vows you are about to take are to be made in the presence of God, who is judge of all and knows all the secrets of our hearts.

Common Worship Marriage Service[9]

The Church also brings a sense of community in the social, public nature of marriage. Weddings take place in church in public and that says something about the communal and legal nature of this new relationship. The Marriage Service pulls no punches in saying that marriage itself 'enriches society and strengthens community'. Marriage is clearly the best framework for the birth and nurture of children, and while we all acknowledge how things can go wrong, we believe marriage is the foundation of family life and that it is in the family that each member can or should 'find strength, companionship and comfort and grow to maturity in love'. It is unfashionable to speak in this way but it is where we are as professional ministers and we need to be confident in proclaiming these virtues. The Church also brings blessing. God blesses what he sees to be good, and most couples come to church for marriage for this simple fact, that they want God to be involved and to approve of their love. We can be really good at this and need to embody this very final act in the wedding process with every response and conversation along the way. The Church is in the business of blessing; we need to be as affirming as God himself is in his love.

A specific role that the priest brings to the wedding process is that of someone trained in liturgy. The liturgy of the Church is deeply rooted, tried, tested and, when prayed with sincerity and exercised with flair, is a wonderful vehicle for celebrating the love of two people and the love of God. However familiar with liturgical practice they may be, couples rely upon the minister to know about options and opportunities within the service and the ways in which their service can be made unique and personal. The priest needs to have complete command of the rubrics, to master both the way in which weddings are best celebrated in their particular church, and the art of making the most of each occasion. All of this is a minimum requirement. As professional worship leaders we ought also to be aware that it is rare for us to receive in-service training for weddings or to have our practice reviewed. Just occasionally the committed priest really ought to care enough to ask a member of the Diocesan Liturgical Committee, the rural dean, or someone who has to conduct a lot of weddings to attend a service to offer constructive criticism. Priests reading this might like to ask themselves when they last had input on leading weddings, bearing in mind that weddings are invariably led by one priest alone. We have the duty to be really effective in the area of liturgical provision, the people expect it of the clergy; it is what we do, so we need to do it well.

Another of the crucial qualities that the professional marriage minister offers is experience. Whether married or not, the priest will have had more experience of weddings than either bride or groom and will be able to advise them with wise counsel. The priest needs to become a trusted friend through this process. Parents and friends have a rather delightful way of unintentionally putting pressure on couples from the moment the wedding is announced. Expectations are high for the 'best day of your life', which actually is also potentially 'one of the best days in everyone else's life' too. A priest needs to be able to say 'no' to obscure requests in a way that shows why such a response is the best option. This means not 'lording it' over couples but being on their side to help them make sensible decisions. Clergy tend to lead more funerals than weddings. At a funeral the task and the care and sensitivity required is obvious. Even if clergy are only taking a few weddings a year, the same care and attention is needed, and perhaps more thoughtful and prayerful preparation is needed if weddings are less frequent. I know I am always less confident and rustier at the first wedding of the season. It is a sign of professionalism to take this into account in the planning process.

The professional marriage minister, the Church of England priest, also brings a unique perspective and contribution. The minister will be one of the few people the couple meet in connection with their wedding who will not be making a profit out of it. The priest–couple relationship is not a commercial one, even though wedding fees are involved. The priest must never cross this boundary in reality or perception. Couples who visit me value this almost without exception and volunteer this information. They speak of how all their other wedding arrangements feel like the buying of a product – this grade of menu or the one lower down if you can't afford that. Couples find in their priest someone they do not come across in society generally, someone who has time for them, someone who cares for them deeply, someone who is prepared to accept them as they are rather than demand that they conform. I knew a parish priest once who had a lot of weddings at his church. After a while, some of us discovered one of the reasons for this. What he looked for by way of a sign of commitment, whether the couple attended regular worship or not, and therefore whether they could be married in church or not, was 'had the couple signed up for planned giving?' While we all hope this might be something a couple undertake once married and committed to the regular congregation, being on the stewardship list is not an acceptable qualification for marriage.

Of course, special to the clergy is the provision of marriage preparation. The obligation for marriage preparation is placed upon the priest who will marry the couple, and this should never be ignored. I heard recently from a bride to be that she had seen her priest to make choices for the wedding, and at the end of the interview she opened her diary to book in further times together, now that detailed arrangements could be left behind. 'When will I see you next, vicar?' was the question. 'Well, at the rehearsal I guess' was the reply. We need though to be careful about the way we use our technical phrase 'marriage preparation'. All couples come to be married in church having begun their marriage preparation already. Almost all couples who come to us are spiritually serious. We may need a better phrase that sets out our offer of teaching and articulation of lifelong commitment in love.

The length, depth and content of marriage preparation will vary from priest to priest and parish to parish. But it should never be this brief! Some may choose to build on the strong foundations of the personal relationship to go through the marriage liturgy in a way that both informs the head and moves the heart, perhaps using it as a way to lead onto further, deeper discussions about the nature of marriage. Others may want to bring couples together to meet with other couples, perhaps involving leadership from within the congregation. There are marriage preparation courses and plans available that can provide a useful framework for further discussion and reflection – see, for example, the material produced by Andrew Body.[10] And as well as marriage preparation, the clergy offer an availability for the rest of a couple's married life. The clergy are rooted in their communities, attached to places of worship that have stood the test of time, and the priest will always grant a (free) interview or visit. Couples often see the priest who married them as having a special place in their marriage just as much as the physical place in which they were married. It is a valuable personal commitment that shows that the Church is there for the long haul, for better, for worse.

Perhaps the most significant contribution by the professional marriage minister is, therefore, this personal relationship between priest and couple. This is the essential relationship that makes a church wedding a success. The priest is to be friend, pastor, teacher, shepherd, worship leader and confidant. If it is the couple who are ministers of the sacrament in marriage, it is the priest who gives them the vocabulary and the vision to understand this. This understanding is important not just for the wedding day itself, but for the whole of their married life together. If husband and wife are 'priests' to each other on their wedding day, they continue in that sacrificial role each and every day for the rest of their lives. This brings a new understanding to their marriage vows, that their commitment to each other is not just a logical decision or a movement of the heart, it is a vocation. Their calling is to be holy for each other and it is in living this way that they discover more and more about the God who continually calls them into relationship with him. The new possibilities for marriage qualification give us the chance to see marriage as a great mission opportunity and the responsibility to ensure that this mission has a powerful impact on each and every couple. I believe that now is the time for clergy and parishes to renew their practice and policy regarding holy matrimony. It is the time to re-commit ourselves, as a Church, to the sacrament of marriage so that it can continue to enrich society and build community. Now is the time to look again at how couples experience us and the service that we provide. I believe we are being led into a new way of working and that the Church can respond with its outward and visible ministry to make a real inward and spiritual impact on couples and our nation as a whole.

The Archbishop of Canterbury has summarized the teaching on marriage for couples in this way.

> For Christians, marriage represents not only an unchanging ideal but forms the bedrock of society. We marry not only because we love, but to be helped to love. Those who commit to each other in marriage do so knowing that they will find support during hard times and enjoy the security and contentment they need to grow and develop as human beings. It is this unconditional presence of comfort and support that sets the foundation for stability and trustworthiness, allowing children to grow up confident that whatever happens there's something fixed and dependable that offers them room, time and space to grow.

> As St Paul teaches us, a husband and wife joined in marriage belong not to themselves, but to each other. By marrying they give over ownership in themselves to another person. And it is this risk – this investing of yourself in another person and letting them invest themselves in you so completely – that is the key to how we grow and become human. As such marriage is for life, as a lifelong commitment undertaken between two people. But it is also 'for life' – as something that fosters and enhances a special kind of human experience.[11]

So we can see, in Scripture, through the sacramental life of the Church and the teaching of our church leaders, that marriage is truly a transformative gift for couples.

5

Getting connected, journeying together

Legislation is hardly the stuff of romantic dreams, unless you are a particular type of lawyer! Having legislation that is aimed at enabling mission might seem equally incongruous but that is what we have, effectively, in the Marriage Measure 2008. I believe the legislation will succeed in its task in opening the doors wider for marriage in church if, and only if, the Church uses the legislation in a way that is 'mission-shaped' and welcoming. This chapter is therefore both about process and good practice. How will the legislation work hand in hand with the Church's mission? What are the keys to a good welcome and effective nurture of couples today? A biblical text goes to the heart of our marriage ministry: the account of the Journey to Emmaus.

> Now on that same day two of them were going to a village called Emmaus, about seven miles from Jerusalem, and talking with each other about all these things that had happened. While they were talking and discussing, Jesus himself came near and went with them, but their eyes were kept from recognizing him. And he said to them, 'What are you discussing with each other while you walk along?' They stood still, looking sad. Then one of them, whose name was Cleopas, answered him, 'Are you the only stranger in Jerusalem who does not know the things that have taken place there in these days?' He asked them, 'What things?' They replied, 'The things about Jesus of Nazareth, who was a prophet mighty in deed and word before God and all the people, and how our chief priests and leaders handed him over to be condemned to death and crucified him. But we had hoped that

he was the one to redeem Israel. Yes, and besides all this, it is now the third day since these things took place. Moreover, some women of our group astounded us. They were at the tomb early this morning, and when they did not find his body there, they came back and told us that they had indeed seen a vision of angels who said that he was alive. Some of those who were with us went to the tomb and found it just as the women had said; but they did not see him.' Then he said to them, 'Oh, how foolish you are, and how slow of heart to believe all that the prophets have declared! Was it not necessary that the Messiah should suffer these things and then enter into his glory?' Then beginning with Moses and all the prophets, he interpreted to them the things about himself in all the scriptures.

As they came near the village to which they were going, he walked ahead as if he were going on. But they urged him strongly, saying, 'Stay with us, because it is almost evening and the day is now nearly over.' So he went in to stay with them. When he was at the table with them, he took bread, blessed and broke it, and gave it to them. Then their eyes were opened, and they recognized him; and he vanished from their sight. They said to each other, 'Were not our hearts burning within us while he was talking to us on the road, while he was opening the scriptures to us?' That same hour they got up and returned to Jerusalem; and they found the eleven and their companions gathered together. They were saying, 'The Lord has risen indeed, and he has appeared to Simon!' Then they told what had happened on the road, and how he had been made known to them in the breaking of the bread.

(Luke 24.13-35)

Short walk, long journey

The Road to Emmaus is a well-known Gospel account. Most regular churchgoers could recount the main points and sequence of events in

the story from memory. We use this Gospel when speaking about
the Christian faith as a journey, when encouraging those growing in
discipleship and when affirming Jesus' presence when we break bread.
This Gospel passage is also helpful when thinking about marriage and,
in particular, for that part of the process when couples approach the
Church about their wedding. It is a good story to bear in mind at
all stages of the process from answering the first phone enquiry
onwards.

Like the two people walking and talking on the way from Jerusalem to
Emmaus, couples have already begun their journey together when they
approach us. It is important for the Church to recognize that this
relationship has been in place for some time and that the first contact
between couple and church is just another staging post on the journey of
their marriage to each other. They have a story to tell, they have been
'talking and discussing' their love for some time and how this might best
be sealed. Hand in hand, they will have talked over how to make that
nervous, 'different from anything they've ever done before', telephone
call or conversation and they won't quite know the right words to use or
how to express what they are asking for. Couples will often ask about
marriage in church in a way that seems right to them but can engender a
less than generous response from the cleric or parish office. This problem
has been exaggerated by the requirements of the previous marriage
legislation. All too often the response to the first enquiry has been a
seemingly negative one about parish boundaries, licences and the
electoral roll. It is not unreasonable that couples wonder why being able
to vote in local and national elections has anything to do with being
married in church! Common phraseology can be confusing: the Register
of Electors (the parliamentary electoral list) is often confused with the
ecclesiastical electoral roll. Just like the two disciples on the way to
Emmaus, new couples know part of the process but they have yet to
understand it. We also need to be wary of labelling people as 'wedding
couples' in a limiting way – perhaps to mean that they come to us with
demands with little long-term commitment in return. We must
remember that wedding couples are people in search of God's love.

On the road to Emmaus, Jesus himself drew near the two people and walked with them. The task of each church, represented chiefly by the priest, is to walk in person with the couple on their continuing journey towards marriage: a journey through which they will come to a greater understanding of Jesus himself. Jesus is inquisitive, asking the two about their story and they are only too happy to tell Jesus what they know. They ask questions and are fascinated about what has gone on in their lives. Couples are often like this. They have a story to tell and they enjoy telling it. Again, all too often, there is a tendency (particularly for busy clergy) to move too swiftly to administrative arrangements rather than spending time getting to know a couple and listening to their most important story. Hearing the story of how a couple met and of their deepening commitment can be great fun and can easily lead into deeper questions such as 'why get married?' and the importance of marriage in church. We have to recognize that couples come to the Church because they often already sense the presence of God in their relationship and they want to acknowledge that publicly. We must not assume that marriage requests are purely culturally determined or hedonistic: God is involved. The Church needs to affirm its belief in this – that despite our systems, laws and structures, because God is a God of love and of relationship, he is busy bringing people into relationship with one another and with himself. The task of the Church, through the ministry of its representatives, is to walk alongside the couple as they are brought to the point where they can ask Jesus to stay with them and at which they recognize him more fully. Jesus was prepared to spend precious, post-resurrection time with the two disciples and to interpret himself and the Scriptures to them. This is a rare opportunity for the couple to do as the two disciples did: to tell their story in the presence of Jesus within his Church. This is a precious and holy moment, perhaps even their hearts might 'burn within them' as they offer them to God, as well as to each other.

Clergy have been heard to say that they prefer baptisms and funerals to weddings, because there is more of a potential for growth or more obvious pastoral need. By their very nature, weddings are, to some extent, ends in themselves and married couples will usually move away from the parish and relocate all their commitments and allegiances. Sometimes there can seem to be little return for the work involved. Such a mindset, though, can be a self-fulfilling prophecy. We need to take our example from Jesus and walk in his way. We need to be confident in the belief that the God, who is love, is both in and behind all this. Marriage 'enriches society and strengthens community'. Marriage preparation and weddings are not for 'my' parish and for the annual return of church statistics, but investments in mission, God's kingdom, society and for ever. This means we need to develop a clear investment policy and a strategy for what lies beyond the 'great day' itself. It is a good and worthwhile thing upon which to spend time and energy. The Emmaus road encounter might have been in unique circumstances, but the example of Christ accompanying the disciples offers a pattern that transfers easily to marriage preparation. Our task is to accompany couples on this short walk through the joy of getting married in church to help them make a safe and enjoyable journey through life in marriage. It must be said that many clergy exercise this ministry in an excellent way; the approval rating among couples after weddings in church is almost 100 per cent. We have much to be proud of and much to build upon.

Two days after their wedding, Greg and Donna knocked on the vicarage door. Back again in jeans and t-shirts, they brought gifts to the priest just to say a heartfelt thank you. The priest had told them that the service would be the best part of their day, and despite all their successful party plans, Greg and Donna had found that she'd been right all along. They left by saying that they would never be the same again and that the church had done its job for them really well.

Their 'Thank You' card said; 'Dear Revd Sue, Thank you so much for everything you have done along our wedding journey. The "process" was lots of fun and everything you discussed with us was so meaningful. Everyone made such positive comments about the beautiful service and how well it all went. Everything about the service was perfect.'

The popular Emmaus course (see e-mmaus.org.uk)[12] helps us see the value of seeing the marriage journey in the context of this Gospel. *Emmaus: The Way of Faith* describes three stages of engagement with enquirers of the faith – contact, nurture and growth. We can treat marriage enquirers in a similar way.

Stage One: CONTACT

This initial period is about establishing contact and building relationships. It requires listening, welcome and companionship.

Stage Two: NURTURE

This is the time for clear information, help with choices and teaching through engagement and marriage preparation. The personal relationship with the priest is built here. The couple are nurtured into a deeper understanding of marriage as they prepare for their wedding.

Stage Three: GROWTH

This is confirmed on the wedding day as the couple experience a transformative spiritual event rather than just an occasion. As they leave changed, to continue their journey as husband and wife, they begin a continuing discovery of each other and of God in their lives that will grow as their marriage deepens. There is the opportunity for reflection after the wedding, the celebration of anniversaries and the availability of ongoing pastoral care.

Couples often approach their marriage with more seriousness than the Church anticipates. They want to learn and to be taught, and come to us expecting to receive some form of marriage preparation. By making contact, in effect, couples have asked us into their lives and all we need to do is to respond faithfully as fellow pilgrims. This is the open door to faith that this rite of passage provides. Couples are open to discovering the spirituality in their wedding and many see this as their chance, once and for all, to respond to God. We may call this an evangelistic opportunity. They see it as God being personally involved in their lives. It probably adds up to the same thing.

Contact – meeting for the first time

It may be stating the obvious to encourage good practice among the clergy when having contact with wedding couples. However, so much hangs on our approach and especially first impressions that it is worth underlining and repeating the message. Wedding couples come forward with such excitement and a sense of importance that this needs to be acknowledged in the response. Even if the clergy have heard it all a hundred times before, this is, we hope, the only time a couple will make such an enquiry. Understandably, speaking to the clergy can be a daunting prospect for couples, but the clergy can be confident in their ability to put couples at ease. Access to clergy, compared with access to many other professionals, is still good and immediate. The couple can actually get to speak to a vicar in person, whether telephoning to a direct line or by calling at his or her home or by turning up in church on a Sunday morning. Such a level of intimacy in business and public service transactions is very rare today. Our ministry is still public and local, and long may it remain so. But clergy can be strange creatures, and media versions of the clergy don't always help (although there *are* some positive role models). So the initial response to a wedding enquiry is crucial – it begins a pastoral relationship. It is important to return calls swiftly and to be in the right frame of mind when returning a call. Clergy are very busy people; better to let the answerphone take the call and reply when there is good time than to reply in a rush.

Despite the pressure of the 'urgent' it is also important to reply promptly too. We must be sure to avoid any 'leakage' just because we are short of administrative time. So when any enquiry is made, the following checklist ought to be in the mind of the church representative:

- an expression of congratulation and welcome

- a reassurance that the church will be able to offer good advice and information

- the importance of approaching marriage in a serious and informed way

- an explanation of the next step, and

- a dedication to God for blessing.

A smile and a handshake go a long way too. It is important not to be trite and to promise anything, especially when there may be as yet undisclosed facts such as a previous marriage, but it is possible to be genuinely welcoming and informative in the same conversation, and to communicate that the Church has a 'can do' culture. It can be great fun to role play this kind of first contact with the PCC and it teaches members of the church what is involved in pastoral situations. Such principles are equally important when the parish telephone number is answered by a parish administrator or official. Training is vital for all those who answer on behalf of the church.

I spoke to Rhiannon Jones, a parish priest and General Synod member from Ely Diocese. Her parish prepares the most wonderful wedding pack. It comes in a nice folder and contains:

- a letter from the vicar, explaining practical things like process and costs

- a selection of possible Bible readings for the service

- a selection of hymns for their 'Big Day' and guidance on choosing hymns

- a glossy pamphlet on preparing for a wedding in church

- two brochures offering free weekends, one for engaged couples and one for married couples, to help strengthen relationships

- a CD to help draft an order of service

- a copy of a bride magazine, with a Foreword by the bishop

- a booklet explaining what Christians believe

- a copy of the Marriage Service

- and, finally, a card from the parish wishing the couple well in their preparations

- and, finally, finally, some heart-shaped chocolates.

One cannot but be impressed by the quality of this welcome and the standard of the ensuing marriage preparation including special days and meals together.

The next most obvious stage is to meet with a couple. Some parishes will have the tradition of a 'parish office hour' or surgery but this can be very impersonal. One parish I knew operated this system, with couples having to sit in a dusty vestry in just the fashion of a dentist's waiting room and wait to be called in to see the vicar. While this might have helped administratively and saved time in a busy urban parish, it didn't offer much to make people feel special or loved by God. There are better ways of organizing couples and weddings. If, as we have said, it is important to hear the couple's own story, then that ought to be the starting point of a first meeting. Getting to know each couple is important. Few parishes can claim that they have so many weddings a year that this is impossible, and if they do, they need to think about how to organize themselves differently in order to maintain quality as well as quantity. Each parish and each priest must find their own solution to this process; however imaginative and innovative the arrangements might be, the principles of good practice remain the same. We bear the responsibility, collaboratively, individually and corporately, to get this right for the Church and for couples alike. The clergy need to be supporting one another in new ways to administer weddings most effectively.

For many clergy, the only space they have for seeing couples is at home in the vicarage. This has big implications for family life and privacy, both for vicarage families and for couples. But it should not be underestimated how powerful a tool the vicarage still is for the church. No other professional invites you to their home. No other professional allows strangers to see the workings of the desk or the pile of un-filed papers. Welcoming couples into the kitchen or sitting room for a coffee is demanding but disarming. Couples are excited by such visits and sit outside in the car waiting for their appointed time – they almost always arrive early for such appointments! There is a clear sense of anticipation in their behaviour – it's been a while since he proposed, and now for the first time, the wedding thing seems really real. There are practical realities. Clergy need to be well organized and ready for the visit, whether at home, or in the vestry or the parish office. Put the telephone answering machine on and stop it ringing all the way through the 30 minutes or so together. There needs to be somewhere to sit comfortably that is not covered by papers for the next Diocesan Synod. Any papers or printed information for the couple need to have been prepared beforehand. Couples really value, and are even taken aback by this hospitality.

It may also be reasonable to visit a wedding couple in their own home rather than in the vicarage. Recently, I visited Chris and Fiona because it was easier to do so when their kids were tucked up in bed. It gave them confidence and they could relax. It seemed right to talk about the commitment of marriage in the place that they live out their current commitment each day.

Nurture – company for the journey

Jesus nurtured Cleopas and the other disciple on the road to Emmaus. For the clergy, what might often seem to be repetitive administration is really exciting news to couples (chapter 8 of *Mission-Shaped Parish* by Paul Bayes and Tim Sledge is worth a read[13]). When conducting such interviews, couples often remark at the end that they are 'really excited now'. As professionals, we have the duty to help each couple feel as if this is as important to the Church as it is to them. As ministers of the gospel, clergy also need to keep before couples the holy aspect of what they are doing as well as the legal process and the planning of choices for a service.

The House of Bishops has issued guidance for the clergy and parishes in finding their way around the Marriage Measure 2008. This guidance is available in full on the Church of England web site.[14]

The purpose of this guidance is to help determine the status of a 'Qualifying Connection' and to describe ways of providing evidence to support such an application for marriage. The guidance emphasizes the importance of offering a welcome to couples who come to the Church for marriage. That is the abiding tone of the advice. So if a couple do not qualify for a wedding in a particular parish church under the Measure, the guidance goes on to stress the responsibility of the minister to discuss with them all other possibilities and, if the couple wish, give help in making contact with a church where they might have such a connection. The importance of marriage preparation is also stressed and the duty to provide such nurture is placed upon the priest taking the wedding. However, if a couple are to marry in a parish under the Measure, yet live too far away to take part in a course of marriage preparation, they should be invited to undertake such preparation in their home parish or deanery. These two principles of the guidance encourage a new way of working for the clergy, again recognizing that marriage in church is a shared responsibility for the whole Church and not just about parochial boundaries.

The main points of the House of Bishops' Guidance are summarized, simplified and paraphrased here to give an overview.

PART I
THE MEASURE

- The Church of England Marriage Measure 2008 extends the existing legal right to be married in a parish to where one or both of the couple can establish a Qualifying Connection with the parish.

- The Measure does not affect the existing rights of parishioners. A couple continues to have the right to be married in the parish church of a parish where one or both of them are resident or entered on the church electoral roll.

- The Measure does not affect the existing position regarding the remarriage of a divorced person whose former husband or wife is still alive.

- The Measure does not affect the procedure for issuing an Archbishop of Canterbury's Special Licence or the principles on which such a licence is granted. Further information about the issue of special licences is available from the Faculty Office of the Archbishop of Canterbury and on its web site at: www.facultyoffice.org.uk

- The Measure does not grant the couple any greater rights than a parishioner would have; for example, the couple do not have the right to insist on being married on a particular date or at a particular time. The date and time have to be agreed with the minister of the church. A marriage must be solemnized within three months after the publication of banns has been completed and between 8 am and 6 pm. The services of an organist, a choir, bell-ringers and other such requests is a matter for agreement.

- All references to attending public worship are confined to services according to the rites of the Church of England.

- The Measure does not apply to any cathedral.

- A marriage under the Measure will normally take place following the publication of banns. The banns must be published where the marriage is to take place and in the parish or parishes where each of the couple is resident.

- It is possible to apply for a Common Licence under the Measure but not a Superintendent Registrar's Certificate.

- An Applicant (one of the persons to be married) is responsible for establishing that he or she has the necessary Qualifying Connection. Thus the Applicant must provide such information, written or otherwise, as the person with statutory responsibility for deciding the matter requires in order to satisfy himself or herself of the connection.

PART II
A: GENERAL GUIDANCE

- The Minister of the parish has a statutory responsibility for deciding whether the information is sufficient to satisfy him or her that there is a Qualifying Connection and whether to ask for a statutory declaration.

- It is important for the Minister to bear in mind that the Measure was passed because the Church wishes to support and encourage marriage, and to provide a welcoming ministry to couples who wish to be married in church.

- There is a standard form available for the application for marriage (see the example in Appendix 2 on pp. 126–37).

- In cases where qualification is not straightforward, the Minister should make every effort to ask for further information and to enable a reasonable register search if required. A range of possible questions around qualification is provided in the House of Bishops' Guidance.

- Where the Minister finds that a case is not straightforward, he or she may consult the Diocesan Registrar, explaining to the couple that further advice is needed about how to proceed, and that the Minister will come back to them once that advice has been received.

- The main types of advice may be that the Minister can agree to the marriage taking place; more information is needed and what it is; or the Minister should require the Applicant to make a statutory declaration, and what information it should cover; or an application for a Common Licence or Special Licence may be more appropriate in the circumstances; or the application to be married under the Measure, following banns should be rejected and on what grounds. The Minister should follow the Registrar's advice and inform the couple accordingly.

- The Minister should not decide to reject an application without obtaining advice from the Diocesan Registrar unless it is clear beyond doubt that none of the Qualifying Connections exists.

- Where the Minister has to reject an application it is good practice for him or her to write to the couple, explaining why this is the case with reference to the law and setting out possible alternatives or seeing the couple in person to do the same and in either case to make it clear to the couple, so far as possible, that the Church is still extending a welcome to them and that a church wedding in a parish where the law permits it to take place is still very much open to them.

- The responsibility for proving the connection lies with the Applicant. The test is always whether the Minister is satisfied that the Qualifying Connection is established.

- The information can be provided in various ways such as:

- ○ the Minister may have personal knowledge of the facts, thereby simply recording these facts on the application, or

- ○ he Minister may have these facts confirmed by another responsible person such as a Churchwarden or Director of Music or

- ○ the Applicant may rely upon information from some other person, which will need to be confirmed in writing.

The information may consist of an entry in a register kept in the parish, which the Minister has seen personally and then a simple record of this is made on the application form. If the information is on a register not seen personally by the Minister, the Applicant must provide a certified copy for the Minister. The Applicant may provide other forms of evidence of residence to satisfy the Minister, and again these facts are to be recorded on the application form.

- The application form must be kept until the date of the marriage. If a statutory declaration has had to be made the application form should be retained and treated like any other confidential document.

B: ESTABLISHING QUALIFYING CONNECTION

- *Baptism* – The Applicant must have been baptized in the parish but not in a combined rite with confirmation where the confirmation is the relevant factor under the Measure.

- This applies to whatever age the Applicant was baptized and in whatever pastoral circumstances (e.g. in emergency). The baptism must have been according to the rites of the Church of England.

- *Confirmation* – A similar rule exists regarding confirmation. The Minister needs to be satisfied regarding the entry in the relevant register.

- *Parent or Grandparent* – a marriage must have taken place according to the rites of the Church of England (i.e. not a civil marriage) according to the marriage register. A parent means: the parent of a legitimate or an illegitimate child, an adoptive parent (legally or a person 'who has undertaken the care and upbringing' of another person). This points to a potentially long-term relationship. For a grandparent, one of the above three types of relationship must apply between each generation and the next, i.e. between grandparent and parent; and between the parent and Applicant.

- The information regarding the marriage should normally be either the entry in a marriage register that the Minister sees personally or a certified copy of a register entry on behalf of the person with the custody of the register.

- The fact that a party to the marriage was the Applicant's parent or grandparent can be established by personal knowledge by the Minister or another person holding office in the parish, birth certificates, certificates of adoption or some form of evidence from a professional person to confirm the claimed status. If in doubt consult both the full House of Bishops' Guidance text and the Diocesan Registrar.

- *Residence* – in order to satisfy this Qualifying Connection, it is necessary to show that the Applicant has at any time had his or her usual place of residence in the parish for at least six months. The same is true for the parent of the Applicant, during the Applicant's lifetime.

- This must have been a 'usual place of residence', that is a 'home base'. This does not include temporary stays for holidays or temporary work.

- It is sufficient to show that one parent satisfies this requirement but not a grandparent.

- The application form should show the address and the Minister must be satisfied that this is in the parish. The application form should state clearly that this was the usual place of residence and in the case of a parent, give the Applicant's date of birth.

- It will often be possible to establish all the elements of the Qualifying Connection together from: the Minister's personal knowledge or that of another holding office in the parish; written information from a former parish priest or independent person, setting out the facts.

- If this cannot be obtained, the Applicant must provide evidence showing residence for the necessary period according to usual forms of identification as listed in the House of Bishops' Guidance.

- The Minister is able to use local knowledge in determining the validity of a 'residence'.

- If, in any case, the Minister is not satisfied by the evidence produced, it may be necessary to require a statutory declaration.

- *Habitual Attendance* – the Applicant or parent has habitually attended public worship in the parish for a period of not less than six months. In the case of a parent, this must have been in the Applicant's lifetime. This does not apply to a grandparent. The form submitted by the Applicant should state where, on what occasions, how often and over what period the Applicant or parent attended worship. The evidence for this can be obtained from the Minister's own experience, a post holder, or a previous priest, post holder or some other independent person.

- *'Habitually'* is not defined by the Measure. It means 'as a matter of habit' and requires an element of habit and regularity. The Minister should regard the test as satisfied if the person concerned has worshipped in the parish over a period of years and regularly attended worship at least three times a year at major festivals, e.g.

Christmas, Easter, Pentecost, Harvest, Remembrance, unless prevented from so doing by illness. Or that the person has attended regularly for six months or more at least once a month unless prevented by illness.

- The worship need not be on Sundays but it must be public worship, that is not school or college worship designated for that purpose and it must be according to the rites of the Church of England.

- The person need not have been an adult or have been baptized. For a young person, this includes attendance as a member of the church choir, as a regular participant in 'church parades' or for a pupil at a school that worshipped regularly as a body at services open to the public say three times a year, so long as the person attended regularly.

- *Electoral Roll* – for any purpose above, a current or past Electoral Roll may be used to provide evidence of qualification; however, there is no obligation on parishes to keep past Electoral Roll documents.

- *Identity* – changing a name can be commonplace. The Applicant is required to provide proof of a change of name or a statutory declaration may be required.

- *Statutory Declarations* – A statutory declaration is a formal declaration, made under the Statutory Declarations Act 1835. It is not made on oath, but knowingly and wilfully making a false declaration is a criminal offence. The declaration must be made before a solicitor with a current practising certificate, a Commissioner for Oaths or a Justice of the Peace, and in most cases a statutory fee will be payable. A specimen form is provided in the House of Bishops' Guidance. The Minister should not require a statutory declaration as a matter of course and should consult the Diocesan Registrar if he or she feels one is required. The need for a statutory declaration will be if the Minister is not satisfied the evidence provided is comprehensive or if the supporting information from a suitable person is not seen to be independent, e.g. if the supporting person is a close relative. The Minister should consult the Diocesan Registrar if there is any doubt as to the best way forward.

- The Minister should retain the declaration after the marriage, in case it is alleged later that the declaration was false and that the person who made it was guilty of an offence.

- *Common Licence* – There are special cases when a marriage needs to be by Common Licence, such as a defect in calling the banns or one of the couple is temporarily resident abroad so that banns cannot be called where he or she is resident. In a case under the Measure, the Applicant must produce sufficient information, written or otherwise, to satisfy the person with authority to grant the licence that he or she has a Qualifying Connection with the parish. The person with authority to grant the licence will normally be a surrogate – an experienced priest in the diocese – or the Diocesan Registrar. A statutory declaration cannot be used under the Measure to support an application for a common licence. A person applying for a Common Licence must make an affidavit, which is made on oath.

PART III
A: WHEN AN APPLICANT IS DIVORCED WITH A SPOUSE STILL LIVING

- As in the case of any marriage where one of the parties has a former spouse still living, a minister is not under a duty to solemnize the marriage or allow his or her church to be used for it. The House of Bishops has already published advice to the clergy on such cases, which applies equally to cases under the Measure. That advice and further information, including a leaflet with an application form for couples, is available on www.cofe.anglican.org/info/papers/mcad

- It is important under the Measure whether the couple have previously approached any other member of the clergy for marriage and if so, why he or she was not willing to marry them. The application process requires this information to be provided by the couple.

B: MARRIAGE PREPARATION

- The minister of the church where the marriage is to be solemnized is under an obligation under Canon Law to explain to the couple the Church's doctrine of marriage and the need for God's grace to discharge their obligations as married people. He or she can and should insist on discussing this with the couple before the marriage, irrespective of how far away from the parish they are living.

- The Minister should give a couple who are to be married in a parish under the Measure every encouragement to undertake whatever further marriage preparation is the usual practice in the parish. The Minister should discuss this with the couple at an early stage, and if they live too far away to take advantage of the marriage preparation arranged in the parish, the Minister should be ready, with their agreement, to contact the parish priest where they or one of them lives to try to arrange for them to undertake marriage preparation there or in another nearby parish.

- It is important for the Minister to agree with the couple at an early stage that, if practicable, he or she will contact the parish priest of the parish where the couple plan to begin married life together and ask him or her to contact the couple, do anything appropriate to support them.

- Previous advice for the marriage of foreign nationals still applies.

Now this long list of guidance, while clear and helpful, may not at first glance feel like 'nurture'. However, each couple come with qualification at the forefront of their minds and they need to feel that this is in place before they can make further arrangements for their wedding. There is a great sense of relief when a couple are told that they qualify for a wedding in the parish church of their choice and a redoubled sense of relief when the date and time are agreed upon. The clergy need to make this new legislation feel like the intention behind it. It is not to be interpreted as a hurdle but a legal framework through which qualification for marriage can be established. The emphasis is as much on the spirit of the law as on the letter of the law. Couples need to be guided through this process with an atmosphere of nurture rather than examination.

Once qualification (or special connection) has been determined, the next stage is to agree a date and time for the wedding. This can often be a challenge, especially when couples come with a specific date in mind and do not realize that the church or the minister may already be booked. Recently I had the sad situation where a couple approached me to book a wedding, with qualification clear as they lived within the parish. Sadly, they had given in to pressure from the reception venue and booked a date (with a hefty deposit) before booking the cathedral. We had a major diocesan event booked for that day and there was no way we could squeeze their wedding in, despite best efforts. Few enough people qualify to be married in the cathedral; this couple did, but their wedding ended up being elsewhere because they had got things in the wrong order. The openness of the new legislation may, over time, help to enable couples to feel that they can approach their parish church with confidence at the earliest possible stage. Couples have no rights over the date and time of their wedding, this is made by agreement. Once this negotiation has taken place the priest can move with confidence into preparing the couple for their marriage service in church. Through this process their relationship will have begun and the couple should have a new friend and pastor in their lives.

Growth – discovering God in the detail of a wedding

The administrative aspect of weddings is also part of the nurture of the couple. The choices made for each wedding, and how these choices are made and informed, can be part of their growth. By working with the priest – their priest – the couple can make detailed choices about the style and content of their service and through this conversation, the couple move from being nurtured to growing in understanding and expectation. Each wedding should be both objective and subjective: objective, in the sense that the liturgy of the Church articulates what we believe about marriage in the public arena and is a given; and subjective in the sense that each wedding is unique and involves the couple concerned, and no other. Every wedding needs to feel and be personal, even if familiar and popular choices are made by different couples.

> Recent research found that couples were looking for weddings that were both 'proper' and 'special'. 'Proper' concerns the traditional and spiritual aspects of the church wedding – the things that resonate with people's deeply held expectations. 'Special' was all about the unique aspects that a couple were able to bring to the wedding to make it unlike any other.[15]

The conversation about hymns, readings, bells, confetti and all the wedding paraphernalia is an important part of the deepening relationship between priest and couple. This conversation needs to be in a positive vein with the priest guiding the couple through positive choices rather than giving negative responses. This is about permission-giving: what can be allowed, enabled and encouraged rather than policing: 'We don't allow that here.' A classic example is confetti. Many churches ask couples not to have confetti thrown at their wedding for reasons of churchyard tidiness and maintenance. If it has to be the case that confetti is not allowed by the PCC then there also needs to be a clear explanation of why that is and also advice as to where confetti *can* be thrown, bio-degradable or not. We are not able to allow confetti at St Albans Cathedral because there are too many other services and visits on the same day (and often at the same time) that would be adversely affected by this joyful activity. So we encourage couples to leave by the West Gate, where, as they climb into their vehicle, confetti is thrown, and blows away harmlessly. We explain that one of the origins of confetti among many is as a sign of their family and friends showering them with prayers as they make their first journey together as husband and wife. It's a bit twee, but it works and the couples comply and feel good about it, having grown a bit through the decision-making process. Every parish will be able to work out what is best for their particular circumstances.

Each parish, team ministry or benefice (whatever seems the right level) needs to agree a policy on wedding choices to clarify things for the couple, to provide a point of reference for the priest, as a good thing to do together and to aid planning. It is best if such a policy is agreed by the parochial church council as it increases a sense of ownership – weddings are, after all, the business of the PCC as well as the priest. There may well be a locally produced leaflet or form with explanatory notes that couples can take away from their first meeting to begin thinking about their wedding choices. This should be accompanied by a clear representation of current fees. Certain times of year may dictate whether a choir or bell-ringers are available and the minister will be able to give this advice. It is through this conversation that the couple will come to trust their priest more and more and be better prepared to discuss more fully the nature of Christian marriage and to engage in marriage preparation. So growth takes place from the moment this conversation begins and it is not purely administrative. The priest may take the opportunity to teach about the faith through the choices couples make, especially through the selection of hymns and readings. Laying the ground for marriage preparation is an important aspect of wedding planning. It is about creating the safe place for growth. This will continue and deepen each time the couple and priest meet, and especially if the couple come to church to hear their banns being read, or respond to the encouragement to come and join in the worship in the place where they are to be married. Prayer and welcome may accompany the reading of banns. A member or members of the congregation can be given the role of welcoming couples, sitting with them through the service and ensuring they feel part of things afterwards. There may also be times of pastoral need in the run-up to a wedding, such as a family member being ill or dying: the priest can use this new relationship to walk with the couple through this time. It is crucial that through this period of planning and relationship the love of God in Christ is represented and made tangible.

Further discussion of parish policy regarding wedding choices by couples and marriage preparation is made in Chapter 7, along with a consideration of further growth opportunities after the wedding.

Growth continues as a bride and groom approach their wedding date. The rehearsal for the wedding is a reality check for the couple and their nearest and dearest. The rehearsal should be simple, informative and fun. The purpose of a wedding rehearsal is not to send the couple away with a set of instructions to remember off by heart but to give them a simple familiarity with what will happen to them in a day or two. It is the priest's job to remember what the couple have to do, not theirs. He or she has conducted a wedding before and is the professional in this situation. The couple are amateurs and need gentle leadership. The rehearsal should be led, questions are best kept for the end and the whole time (45 minutes is ample) should begin and end with a short prayer. Photographers and videographers can be invited along to see how the service will be presented in a particular church and the priest can take the opportunity to brief them, again by saying what is allowed in a positive way rather than what is not allowed. Photographers respond better to clear, concise, enabling information rather than simply being told what they can't do.

The greatest point of growth for the couple is the wedding day itself and the marriage service. If the priest has done his or her job well, the couple will look back on their day, with all its carefully laid plans and napkin-folding arrangements, and say that the best part of the day for them was the service. The task of the priest is to celebrate the wedding so that the bride and groom are literally changed by what they say and do to each other and by what God does with them. Participating in a moving wedding changes couple and congregation alike. The wedding needs to be an act of worship and not just the first event of a long and expensive day. The wedding, and not the reception, needs to set the tone for the whole celebration and be the climax of the couple's preparations. God can use a wedding to help us all grow in faith – we are partners with him in this mystery. It is to the celebration of the wedding liturgy itself that the next chapter turns.

6

Celebrating marriage

> On this their wedding day the bride and bridegroom face each
> other, make their promises and receive God's blessing. You are
> witnesses of the marriage, and express your support by your
> presence and your prayers. Your support does not end today: the
> couple will value continued encouragement in the days and years
> ahead of them.
>
> *Common Worship: Pastoral Services*, Pastoral Introduction[16]

This is a job description. It says what we are doing in the liturgy of the
Marriage Service. It is about the couple, the people present, God and
his blessing. It looks as much to the future as to the present moment. Of
all the services in *Common Worship*, the liturgy of the Marriage Service is
the least changed from that of the *Alternative Service Book 1980* and from
the rites that immediately preceded it. The Marriage Service stands as
an example of the value of the sacramental moment and the common
understanding of the Church. It is important not only that the
professional marriage minister knows what he or she is doing with it but
also that the couple, in each and every case, understand what is being
done to them and with them. This chapter therefore naturally falls into
two main parts: first, the communication of the meaning of the Marriage
Service to the couple and secondly, the content and delivery of the
service from the minister's point of view.

Talking about the Marriage Service with the wedding couple

Nearly 25 years ago, my wife and I must have been among the last, I hope, to have received marriage preparation that consisted solely of the 'birds and the bees' talk and the selection of old wives' tales that passed for good advice. But what did work for us, and made a lasting impression, was the teaching we received about the content and meaning of the Marriage Service. This, more than anything, prepared us for the day and has made a difference ever since. Knowing within our hearts what we were doing, and why we were doing it in church, made our day. And, in those days, we were not 'churchy'. So when preparing couples for marriage, the first duty of the priest has to be to teach about the meaning of marriage as expressed within Scripture and the service – the liturgy within which their marriage will be made real and effective. If we cannot bring something distinctive to the marriage party through the liturgy then we have nothing to bring other than tradition and 'bling'. Every time I sit down with a wedding couple, I insist on taking them through the service word for word. This is where marriage preparation really begins.

Perhaps a month or so before the wedding date is a good time to arrest the wedding bandwagon and teach about the content of the service. This is not really the place for questions that will come up at the rehearsal but a 'stand-alone' time when the priest moves from the roles of administrator, registrar and receptionist to those of pastor, teacher and friend. The couple should have previously been given a copy of the Marriage Service to read over and ponder together.[17] Then is the time for sitting together over coffee to discuss the content of the service. The couple may be silent for much of this 'conversation', but that is usually because they are taking it all in, and the real development comes when they talk it over again with each other in the pub afterwards or during the coming days.

Many clergy will have their own unique and powerful ways of communicating this liturgy to couples. All that follows in this chapter is what I use when I engage in this vital conversation, adapted over the years in response to invaluable feedback from couples and reflecting my own personal style.

It should be remembered that couples are free to choose any of the Church of England's three authorized marriage rites: that in *The Book of Common Prayer* (1662), the Series One service,[18] or the *Common Worship* rite, and that these options should be discussed with them. This book focuses on the *Common Worship* Marriage Service.

The first task is to spend a moment looking at the structure of the service so that couples can grasp the overall shape of what it is that we are doing together with God.

The Marriage Service – structure

Introduction

> The Welcome
>
> Preface
>
> The Declarations
>
> The Collect
>
> Readings
>
> Sermon

The Marriage

> The Vows
>
> The Giving of Rings
>
> The Proclamation
>
> The Blessing of the Marriage
>
> Registration of the Marriage
>
> Prayers
>
> The Dismissal

Talking through this structure and giving the couple an overview before they become immersed in detail is important. It helps couples to see the shape of the service and how the first part of the liturgy is an essential preliminary to what they will be doing in the second section, much as their engagement has been a build-up to the real thing. It also helps give substance to the idea that the structure of the service has to do with stages on a journey. (The *Common Worship* rite also allows for the Sermon or the Readings and Sermon to come after the Blessing of the Marriage.)

Introduction

The Welcome

It can be explained that this section is a formal welcome – expressed through the words of the Grace – both of the couple and their invited guests. This Trinitarian greeting is significant, making it clear from the outset that we are engaging in a holy activity and that God is present. The sentence from 1 John 4.16, 'God is love, and those who live in love live in God and God lives in them', expresses at the outset our understanding of the God who calls us into relationship with him. Some couples can be encouraged to learn this simple biblical phrase off by heart for use in their prayers as they prepare to be married, and it is surprising how many take this up.

The prayer that follows affirms the fact that the couple recognize the need for God's involvement in their lives and that they need his inspiration to reach their full potential.

> God of wonder and of joy;
>
> grace comes from you,
>
> and you alone are the source of life and love.
>
> Without you, we cannot please you;
>
> without your love, our deeds are worth nothing.

Send your Holy Spirit,

and pour into our hearts that most excellent gift of love,

that we may worship you now

with thankful hearts

and serve you always with willing minds;

through Jesus Christ our Lord.

Amen.

This prayer looks both at the present moment and to the future, pointing to the nature of our relationship with God as a good model for husband and wife. We 'worship . . . now with thankful hearts and serve . . . with willing minds'. Marriage has to do with both head and heart. People fall in love not because it is a rational decision but because the heart tells us to do so. The mind can help us make the right decisions as we travel through marriage, for better, for worse.

Preface

The Preface is long and detailed. Talking it through with couples is absolutely vital if it is not simply to 'wash over' them on the day, because here is a distilled statement about the nature of Christian marriage. The text is broken up here to illustrate how it might be discussed with couples. The couple should have a copy of the service in their hands.

In the presence of God, Father, Son and Holy Spirit,

we have come together

to witness the marriage of *N* and *N*,

to pray for God's blessing on them,

to share their joy

and to celebrate their love.

The couple have made a decision to be married in the presence of God, in church, and that says as much about them as it does about God. They could have been married almost anywhere these days, but it had to be in church. This says something about their faith, no matter how well or how poorly they may be able to articulate that faith. It had to be in church. It's also a public event, which is important in itself. At St Albans Cathedral, most weddings take place in the beautiful Lady Chapel. The public can and do watch from the Shrine of St Alban, with faces peering through to see the bride. There can often be 50 people just watching the proceedings from this, the best seat in the house. We often get the happy couple to turn and wave hello to the public, who then feel as if they are themselves participants: a wedding is a public event. The Preface goes on to state that the guests are witnesses of that – weddings have a legal dimension – and that they are there to pray for the couple and to ask God's blessing on them – the spiritual dimension. The words to 'share in their joy and celebrate their love' remind us of the party afterwards! It is easy to talk couples through this short list to show the reasons why we are there in church and they can identify with all these priorities for them and for their families.

> Marriage is a gift of God in creation
>
> through which husband and wife may know the grace of God.
>
> It is given
>
> that as man and woman grow together in love and trust,
>
> they shall be united with one another in heart, body and mind,
>
> as Christ is united with his bride, the Church.

While Christian marriage is not the only form of marriage, the institution of marriage itself is a gift of God in creation – something born out of God's love and through which we come to know God more deeply. Man and woman grow together in love and trust; they are not the 'finished article' at the end of their wedding day, they are beginning a life together through which they will grow both as a couple and as individuals. Through marriage, they will be united: in heart, body and mind. The order here is not insignificant. Traditionally, in Jewish thought, and therefore within the wider Christian tradition, the heart has been seen as the place of true decision-making. This is still evident in some of the ways in which people speak; think of the expressions 'follow your heart' or 'let your heart decide'.

The concept of Christ as 'bridegroom of the Church' is one that it is hard to communicate. What is crucial in the context of marriage preparation, though, is to get across the nature of Christ's love for the Church – that it is a love of total self-giving (cf. Philippians 2.5-11) – which led him to lay down his life for those whom he loved. ('No one has greater love than this, to lay down one's life for one's friends' John 15.13.) This *agape* love is what should stand at the centre of a Christian marriage, with each partner seeking the good of the other without limit.

> The gift of marriage brings husband and wife together
>
> in the delight and tenderness of sexual union
>
> and joyful commitment to the end of their lives.
>
> It is given as the foundation of family life
>
> in which children are [born and] nurtured
>
> and in which each member of the family, in good times
>   and in bad,
>
> may find strength, companionship and comfort,
>
> and grow to maturity in love.

Delight and tenderness. It's very good to know that the Marriage Service can celebrate sex and tell us that we are allowed to enjoy it! But as with so many parts of the liturgy, there is another side to this. With the joy of delight comes the responsibility of tenderness. As we enjoy the other person intimately in marriage, so we also have an equal responsibility to care for them. Sex is a powerful force in a relationship and can be used as an expression of deep affection, attraction and commitment but also as a means to *take* rather than to *give* and to use as a way to score points. We also see here in the liturgy the first of several references to, and hints at, the fact that this marriage is for life. We make this unique and exclusive commitment to each other for ever. Marriage is also, clearly, and without compromise, the foundation of family life. None of this means that marriage automatically makes for happy families and is the answer to all relationships under God. It is, however, the means God has given us to provide a suitable framework into which children can be born and nurtured. The Preface pulls no punches though. There are not many liturgies that use the word *bad*. Marriage is an act of *commitment*, not a panacea to all that life might throw at us. It is in living within this commitment that couples can find the strength, companionship and comfort needed for each individual to grow. The references to children also provide an opportunity here to discuss the desire for children and to talk over the challenges of having a family (or finding that one cannot have a family) in a safe conversational environment.

Marriage is a way of life made holy by God,

and blessed by the presence of our Lord Jesus Christ

with those celebrating a wedding at Cana in Galilee.

Marriage is a sign of unity and loyalty

which all should uphold and honour.

It enriches society and strengthens community.

No one should enter into it lightly or selfishly

but reverently and responsibly in the sight of almighty God.

Marriage has been around for a while and may take many forms but God has made Christian marriage holy and, through his son at Cana, he has got involved with it himself. This reference gives the opportunity to discuss the richness of this Gospel passage or to send the couple away to consider it at home. Marriage also commands respect – something important to hold on to in a society that can be unduly cynical about marriage. Though an exclusive relationship, it has a role in society and concerns others as well as husband and wife. Marriage is – as we used to call my last car – an 'honourable estate' and needs mature consideration and serious preparation.

> *N* and *N* are now to enter this way of life.
>
> They will each give their consent to the other
>
> and make solemn vows,
>
> and in token of this they will [each] give and receive a ring.
>
> We pray with them that the Holy Spirit will guide
>
> > and strengthen them,
>
> that they may fulfil God's purposes
>
> for the whole of their earthly life together.

Say the couple's names as you read this text aloud. This may be commonplace to the minister but it sends a tingle down the spines of the couple in question when they hear their names spoken. Entering a way of life is 'portal' language. Through the portal of marriage, we move from one room to another; it is literally a rite of passage, from one state of being to another. It is important to remind couples that they will be giving their consent to be married: this can come in handy when they begin to regret it later! They make solemn vows, which God takes more seriously than the multiplicity of weak and empty promises that we bandy around each day. Vows still matter. Whoever is actually buying their wedding rings, those rings stand for their gift of each other to each other. This is contractual and demands discipline; the ring provides a reminder when we might be tempted to forget our vows. The members of the congregation are then reminded that they are to pray for the couple, both there at the wedding and subsequently. The Holy Spirit will guide and strengthen the couple, not 'do it' for them but work alongside them and give the direction and energy they need to make the marriage work. If the couple commit and respond to this, and are open to the Spirit, they will be sharing in what God wants for them. Once again, we are reminded of the lifelong nature of marriage – it is 'for the whole of their earthly life together'. Many couples will come from families where a divorce has taken place and while the Church recognizes that marriages sometimes do not succeed, we still affirm that marriage is for life and that has to be the intention of the couple themselves.

The Declarations

Now the wording gets a bit legal. This section has participants that include the State, the Church, the couple as individuals and their families and friends. Couples are always fascinated by the reasons somebody might object to the marriage, as they so often do on television. Their friends will be promising them that they will object, but in real life they never do. The four reasons why someone might legally object to a wedding are:

- if the couple are too closely related;

- if one of the couple is under age;

- if one of the couple is already married;

- if one of the couple is not a British citizen (unless the proper permission has been given for the marriage of a foreign national).

More importantly, the next paragraph asks something of the couple rather than the general public.

> The vows you are about to take are to be made in the presence of God, who is judge of all and knows all the secrets of our hearts.

This is good old-fashioned language with somewhat scary references to the God who knows and sees everything. But there is a real seriousness here. The couple should see these words that are going to be said to them as an encouragement to deal with any issues between them that are unresolved or from their individual past. It can be used as an encouragement for reconciliation or confession before the great day. Essentially, this is an opportunity for the bride and the groom to reassure each other that there are no secrets between them now that will divide them later.

The Declarations (with identical words for each person) express each person's consent for what they are about to do. I remind couples that the simple, five-letter phrase 'I will' contains huge significance for them. This statement is effective not just on their wedding day but every day of their marriage. Every morning begins with another 'I will' either as ongoing commitment or the personal conviction to try harder. To have the state of mind that you are in this marriage because you have agreed to it and go on wanting to be in it is fundamental to the success of a marriage. This is equally significant for those who have come to support them. If these commitments are to mean anything at all, they need to be reflected upon. What will the 'We will' of the people mean for the couple? Have they considered this, discussed it, thought about what it will mean and look like in practice? For just as marriage is an exclusive relationship, so it is also one set in community.

The Collect

The Collect can be used by the couple in preparation before the service. They can be encouraged to change the wording to read: 'Pour out your blessing on *us* that *we* may be joined in mutual love and companionship, in holiness and commitment to each other.' I find that couples seem to use this more than one might first expect and it has a greater impact when used in the course of the service on the wedding day.

Readings

Peter Moger, National Worship Development officer, writes:

Chapter 4 addressed some of the themes that can be drawn out from the account of the Wedding at Cana (John 2.1-11), a passage to which couples might relate on several levels. All too often during preparation, though, we focus only on the reading(s) chosen by the couple for their particular service. The Bible contains a rich resource of texts across a range of genres, all of which can help speak to couples as they prepare. It's a good idea to give couples a copy of the *Common Worship Marriage Service* booklet (i.e. the separate) or, failing that, to print off for them from the Church of England web site or from *Visual Liturgy*, the full selection of suggested marriage readings. The value of discussing a range of biblical texts is considerable: couples value the rare opportunity to sit down with a minister of the gospel and learn from Holy Scripture.

The choice of readings is something that needs to be undertaken with care and on which guidance will almost always need to be given, with time taken to explain the meaning of passages. *Common Worship* allows for up to three biblical readings (Old and New Testament, Psalm and Gospel) but, in most cases, one or two will suffice. Couples will often ask whether they may include a poem or non-biblical reading. The inclusion of such items is at the discretion of the minister, and a difficult balance of theological rigour and pastoral sensitivity will often be needed in coming to a decision. If a non-biblical reading is included, it should precede the reading(s) from the Bible; Scripture has the last word.

Music: Careful choice of readings is important, but music is also a crucial part of most wedding celebrations and can make or mar the occasion. In churches with an able choir and organist there is considerable scope for creativity, but in some places resources (both human and instrumental) are limited. Couples will sometimes have done research and have 'chosen' voluntaries for the processions in and out of church. It is crucial that ministers have a realistic understanding of what will 'work' in the local situation,

and be prepared to offer guidance as necessary.
Couples will often have had little experience of singing
hymns and songs since their schooldays (and much less
now than a generation ago), and might need skilful
guidance in choosing appropriate items. Many ministers
will have suffered an overdose of 'All things bright and
beautiful', 'Give me joy in my heart', 'One more step' and
'Jerusalem' over the years! The 'Top 20 Wedding Hymns'
list at www. yourchurchwedding.org is a helpful place to
start. This list includes some 'seasoned favourites' as well as
some excellent newly written words to well-known tunes.
Couples sometimes need to be discouraged from certain
choices, simply because local musical resources will not do
them justice: a hymn that sounds majestic in a large church
can sound faintly comical when accompanied on a
harmonium. If a couple are insistent on choosing a particular
hymn, it can be worth while to spend some time discussing
its meaning during preparation, or even weaving it into the
fabric of the sermon. However, the default position for
clergy regarding the whole approach to helping couples
with hymn and music selection should always be that the
answer is 'yes' if it possibly can be. This is their wedding.

Sermon

I will say more about the Sermon later but, in preparation, it is best
simply to give reassurance that it will not be too long or boring and
provides an opportunity for informal words among many formal words.

The Marriage

The Vows

The couple stand before the minister. From her father, another person
or simply from herself, the minister receives the bride's right hand and

places it in the right hand of the groom so that they join hands. Hands are important in weddings. Hands are symbolic. They are held for comfort and affection and for safety. Hands are used to seal a contract. They are used to reassure and to bless. Hands matter because they are often the first point of contact and the part of us that can lead us astray. We speak of 'clean hands and a pure heart'. We speak of 'having one's hands dirty' with guilt. The joining of hands therefore is not just a simple or liturgical act; it symbolizes all that we do in our daily lives, the decisions we make and the actions that follow. So while the words of the vows are crucially important, so is what we do at this point in the service. Actions can speak louder than words. Hands both deal with the practical, everyday things of life and stand for the deeper, more meaningful content of relationships. The joining of hands and the exchange of vows are the outward and visible signs of the sacrament of marriage; the inward and spiritual grace is the joining of souls. The person making the vow holds the hand of the other.

> I, N, take you, N,
>
> to be my wife/husband,
>
> to have and to hold
>
> from this day forward;
>
> for better, for worse,
>
> for richer, for poorer,
>
> in sickness and in health,
>
> to love and to cherish,
>
> till death us do part;
>
> according to God's holy law.
>
> In the presence of God I make this vow.[19]

The vows are, for most people, the high point of the Marriage Service.

There are statements that declare what is happening: 'to be my wife/ husband', 'from this day forward', 'till death us do part'. Then there are those dual and contrasting commitments: 'to have and to hold', 'for better, for worse', 'for richer, for poorer'. And then there are commitments the like of which the couple will never have made before, such as: 'in sickness and in health'. It is invaluable to spend time with each couple trying to work out with them what they think these words mean for them, both now and in the future. Couples should be encouraged to read the vows both together and on their own in order to meditate and reflect upon them so that the words and their value seep into their soul and are not just a paragraph said once and never considered again before or after the wedding day. It can also be noted, however obvious, that these vows are made both in God's presence and at a public service, so they carry not just the intent of the couple but also the witness of others.

The Giving of Rings

The prayer that accompanies the giving of the rings is one of the best in the *Common Worship* Marriage Service because 'it does what it says on the tin'. It is important to be able to teach couples what rings are for – 'symbol(s) of unending love and faithfulness', and what they do – 'remind them of the vow and covenant which they have made this day'. The rings are the gift from one to another (regardless of who has paid for them) and they are placed on the left hand to recognize the duality in us again, to be able to choose right from wrong. We are constantly asked to make the choice between good and evil, and the ring serves as a reminder when we are apart from our marriage partner. The words that accompany the giving of the rings reflect both the ownership of the other person and the ownership of all that we have: our goods and our bodies. The rings illustrate status and also remind us of that status when we waver. If a ring is lost, encourage the couple to buy another and to return to church to have it blessed. One of my grooms lost his wedding ring on honeymoon – he was in big trouble!

The Proclamation

> In the presence of God, and before this congregation,
>
> *N* and *N* have given their consent
>
> and made their marriage vows to each other.
>
> They have declared their marriage by the joining of hands
>
> and by the giving and receiving of rings.
>
> I therefore proclaim that they are husband and wife.
>
> *The minister joins their right hands together and says*
>
> Those whom God has joined together let no one put asunder.

This dramatic moment is a summary of what has taken place. It is a list, which can be used with the couple to summarize for them what has happened up to this point in the service. It can also be used to re-enforce the teaching that it is the couple who have made the marriage happen; up until this point the minister could have been seen simply as 'master of ceremonies'. They are proclaimed husband and wife before the priest has blessed them. Once they are, in the eyes of the Church, husband and wife, the Church immediately acts to seal this new covenant. In joining their right hands together (hands again!) the priest can wrap his/her stole around their hands as a sign of God's approval and hope for them. They literally 'tie the knot'. Couples like to see in their learning that some of the more folksy phrases and traditions have holy content and foundation.

The Blessing of the Marriage

The Church then acts through the ministry of the priest to pray for God's blessing through the wonderfully generous prayer of nuptial blessing.

> Blessed are you, O Lord our God,
>
> for you have created joy and gladness,

pleasure and delight, love, peace and fellowship.

Pour out the abundance of your blessing

upon N and N in their new life together.

Let their love for each other be a seal upon their hearts

and a crown upon their heads.

Bless them in their work and in their companionship;

awake and asleep,

in joy and in sorrow,

in life and in death.

Finally, in your mercy, bring them to that banquet

where your saints feast for ever in your heavenly home.

We ask this through Jesus Christ your Son, our Lord,

who lives and reigns with you and the Holy Spirit,

one God, now and for ever.

Amen.

The phrase 'Pour out the abundance of your blessing' has an overflowing element to it that makes couples smile when it is pointed out to them that this is God's response to their marriage. This was what they were hoping for when they first contacted the vicar and started worrying instead about qualifying connections. This prayer, with its striking 'visual' language, seems to accord with modern couples, referring to realities of life, such as work, sleep and death. The reference to the 'crown upon their heads' comes from the Eastern tradition and the final section referring to the 'banquet' moves the couple on from Cana to what they might really hope for, a place in heaven with God, at home. When all this is explained to couples I find there is a sense of awe and wonder in them. The mystery is beginning to unfold for them. Wonderful.

The Registration, Prayers and The Dismissal

These final sections need little teaching with the couple. The signing of the registers is a largely practical exercise on behalf of the State. The prayers are a time of intercession for the couple and are the natural response to everything that has gone before. Couples should read through the prayers before the day though and they can make additions or alterations to suit their need. The final general blessing asks God – Father, Son and Spirit – to make us all strong in faith and love, defend us all and guide us all in his name.

The priest and the marriage liturgy

It is the pleasure, the duty and the task of every minister to ensure that the liturgy of marriage is celebrated with equal care, importance and enthusiasm in every wedding. As professionals, we have a duty not only of care but of proclamation of the gospel in what we do and say. The spiritual discipline of ministry requires those of us who conduct weddings regularly to remember that though it may be our one hundredth wedding this year, for the couple it is their number one wedding. This is a first for the couple and a shop window for mission: God is here in this service and it is all too easy for the minister to get in his way. Some of what follows is blindingly obvious and if priest or parish takes such good practice as a norm – as many do – then all well and good. But if priest and parish take the liturgy for granted, we are failing ourselves, failing the couple and failing God. Please read on with the benefit of knowing your own church(es) and local customs but also use this checklist as a way of testing your own practice.

The rehearsal

- This is an important but informal time together, usually in the week running up to the wedding day. It should be encouraging and aimed to put anxieties at rest.

- The purpose of the rehearsal is to make the couple familiar with the liturgy, to rehearse their speaking parts and so that they can feel confident in the leadership by the priest.

- Anyone can come. The minimum number needed for the rehearsal is two, bride and groom, but parents and attendants may come also. It is good if the best man and chief bridesmaid can come too, along with whoever is to 'give the bride away'.

- The rehearsal should start and end with a simple prayer.

- Photographers and videographers may attend to see in slow motion what will happen in the liturgy and this provides an opportunity for briefing them. (Be sure to check first whether their attendance costs the couple an additional fee.)

- Encourage the couple to be on time for the service.

- Discover whether the couple want just their first names used throughout the service and/or full Christian names used for the Vows.

- Show the couple their registers to ensure they are correct.

- Assure the couple of your prayers before their wedding.

Before the service

- The couple can be prayed for by name during the intercessions in the services on the Sunday before the wedding and invited to attend.

- The church building should be clean, ready and open in very good time. People tend to arrive early for weddings and yet take their seats often at the last minute.

- The registers should have been made available.

- Printed orders of service should have been delivered to the church beforehand or brought to the rehearsal. Specific copies for priest, couple, attendants, organist and any other key persons should be in place.

- Sound systems should be checked before people start to arrive.

- Seating and kneelers should be in place.

- The entrance to the church should be clear of litter.

- Ensure that toilets are clean – (we get more comments about this than anything else).

- If applicable, reserved parking spaces for agreed vehicles should be in place early.

- Ushers need to be briefed according to local custom; they value briefing and should not be ignored.

- While local practice will apply, candles on the altar would normally be lit.

- The minister should welcome and brief the congregation before the bride arrives, introducing himself or herself by name. This announcement can be used for any notices regarding photography, confetti and the like but also to encourage the people to join in with the service, pointing out especially the time in The Declarations where they are asked to respond with the words **'We will'**, which are printed in bold type. They should respond, quite literally, boldly. This time of coaching should always be couched in a positive, welcoming tone and can end with an invitation to silent prayer for the couple or, if it is printed within an order of service, to read the Pastoral Introduction.

During the service

- Notes to the Marriage Service are on pages 132ff. of *Common Worship: Pastoral Services*.

- The positions of bride and groom and attendants, when standing and seated, should have been thought through, rehearsed and organized so that the congregation can see the couple as much as possible.

- If the bride is wearing a veil, she should be asked beforehand when she wishes to have it placed back. The options are: (1) on meeting the groom; (2) after the Blessing of the Marriage. She might also need to hand her flowers to a bridesmaid.

- The minister should welcome the people warmly and can use informal words, but always mentioning the couple by name.

- Hymns should be announced.

- Posture – although local custom will dictate, the following is suggested as good practice for the congregation and couple. Simple invitations to stand or sit accordingly should be given.

Service	People	Couple
The Welcome	*Stand*	*Stand*
Preface	*Sit*	*Stand*
Declarations	*Sit*	*Stand*
For **'We will'**	*Stand*	*Stand*
Collect	*Stand*	*Stand*
Readings	*Sit*	*Sit*
Sermon	*Sit*	*Sit*
The Vows	*Sit*	*Stand*
Giving of Rings	*Sit*	*Stand*
Proclamation	*Stand*	*Kneel*
Blessing	*Stand*	*Kneel*
Registration	*Sit*	*Sit*
Prayers	*Kneel*	*Kneel*
Dismissal	*Stand*	*Kneel*

- Preface – a powerful moment as it is read aloud with sensible gravitas. An alternative following the *ASB* text is on page 136 of *Common Worship: Pastoral Services*.

- The Declarations – when speaking to the people look over and through the couple. When speaking to the couple, look directly at them.

- The speaking parts of the couple need to be as loud and as clear as is possible for them. They are facing away from the people so they probably need to be encouraged to speak a bit louder than they think is normal as it makes such a difference to the liturgy if the people can hear them.

- Readings – the readers can be introduced by name as they come forward.

- Sermon – the *Common Worship* Marriage Service requires that a sermon or homily be preached. This is the ideal opportunity for the minister to place this marriage in the context of Scripture and tradition and to personalize the service. The preacher should have in mind the make-up of the congregation, and not preach for too long. I once knew a priest who always used the same analogy for wedding sermons. The choir knew it off by heart and it became a source of ridicule. Use each couple as the resource and inspiration for a sermon and yet be sensitive to their fragility on the day. The preacher should not give the best man's speech. The sermon is the opportunity to teach the couple and the congregation about the gift of marriage in Christ.

- 'Giving Away' – most brides still wish to be 'given away' in some way but this is optional. This need not be done by her father but may be by her mother, another family member or a friend. The words used by the minister are: 'Who brings this woman to be married to this man?' There is no verbal response – that happens only on television. The presenting person gives the bride's right hand to the minister who places it in the bridegroom's right hand. Their hands may need a bit of management!

- Alternatively, after the bride and groom have made their declarations, the minister may ask the parents of the bride and bridegroom in these or similar words: '*N* and *N* have declared their intention towards each other. As their parents, will you now entrust your son and daughter to one another as they come to be married?' Both sets of parents respond: 'We will.'

- The bride and bridegroom should face each other as far as possible for the vows. I have found that they can say their vows much better to each other if they repeat line by line after the minister. If they are up to it, couples can, of course, learn their vows off by heart and say them to each other, but it is important that this is their decision as an error can be embarrassing. A card with the vows printed in 20pt type should be available just in case. It can be very moving when couples say vows from memory to each other, but the whole service ought not to be dominated by their nervousness about getting this part of the service right. There are alternative words for the vows (on page 150 of *Pastoral Services*). The minister may also need to prompt bride or groom if nerves take over.

- Rings are best placed by the best man on to the (flat) page of the minister's service book. Again, hands may need some management.

- The proclamation should be said in a tone of voice that literally 'proclaims' the marriage.

- The priest's stole may be wrapped around the joined hands of the couple, if possible in view of the people. The priest continues to wear the stole while this is done and holds their hands with the stole while speaking the appropriate words.

- During the Blessing, the priest may place his or her right hand on the head of the bride and bridegroom (beware of tiaras and hair gel). Immediately after the Blessing and before the Registration I choose to stand the couple up, and invite the bridegroom to kiss his bride. It isn't in the rubrics of the service but it is only right and proper and engenders an opportunity for applause.

- The Registration should be completed in full view of the congregation. The signing of the registers can also take place at the end of the service but this often feels like a dry ending to the time in church. It's much better to sign and then return to prayer.

- Prayers may be said by the minister or any other person, following the provision on pages 112–13 or from pages 156–68. The couple may also prepare their own prayers with the help of the minister.

- Following the Dismissal the minister ensures the bride has her flowers; the groom has his top hat if he has one, and that the leaving is managed according to an agreement most likely made at the rehearsal. This aspect is often forgotten and it is a great pity if couples don't know what to do or where to go as the first act in their marriage. Leaving church needs to be rehearsed as much as coming up the aisle.

After the service

- Ushers, suitably briefed, can help return the church to order; they like to help.

- They can manage any lost property.

- If there are photographs outside church, the priest may like to go and say farewell to the couple.

- Clergy must make their own judgement about attending wedding receptions if invited. Often, a short visit is hugely appreciated.

- The marriage of the couple can be recorded in the parish magazine and a copy sent to the couple.

- The couple should receive an invitation to attend church on their first anniversary, which is often a Sunday if their wedding has been on a Saturday. One of their hymns from the wedding could be used at that service.

It should be remembered that *Common Worship* provides other resources around the Marriage Service. These are:

- Prayers at the Calling of the Banns

- The Marriage Service within a Celebration of Holy Communion

- Supplementary Texts

- An Order for Prayer and Dedication after a Civil Marriage

- Thanksgiving for Marriage.

Videos at weddings

The use of video recordings at weddings is commonplace. Each parish needs to determine a policy regarding the most appropriate use of a video recording in their church. This needs to be accompanied by clear information and often a signed agreement form between the couple and the parish. For me, a video falls into the area of personalizing a wedding for the couple and so I see it as my duty to enable the use of a video to get the best compromise between the desires of the couple, the aspirations of the videographer and the requirements of the parish. When the use of videos is approached in a positive and constructive manner, I find that couples are keen to maintain the sense of an act of worship over that of a film set.

Formal copyright information regarding the use of video recordings can be found at www.cofe.anglican.org/worship/downloads/litcopy.rtf

The Weddings Project (see pp. 110–11) makes a case for allowing videos, if the videographer has professional qualifications.

Top tips for good wedding videography

Why say 'yes'?
There could be a **marriage care advantage** to agreeing to a

couple's request to have their wedding filmed. They will be able to review their big day and the promises they made, including the highlights of the message you preached. It will make an inspirational keepsake.

Check it out
It's good to have an indication that the videographer **is suitably qualified**, for example has membership of a professional trade association like www.iov.co.uk Make sure they've got all the necessary copyright permissions too. Their expertise, and yours, will ensure everything goes smoothly.

Get together
Contact the videographer (and photographer) before the wedding day. Spending a little **time discussing** the wedding can pay dividends in terms of good order on the day. The wedding rehearsal can be the ideal time to get together.

In your face?
Advanced **light-enhancing technology** means that you don't have to be in people's faces to film close up. Professional videographers will be able to suggest camera positions for maximum visual quality and minimum intrusion.

Under your feet?
If Hollywood is coming to film, expect miles of cabling. But for a wedding filmed for personal use, **built-in batteries** are standard on modern cameras. So tripping up is less of an issue.

How many cameras are too many?
It's not unusual to have three cameras film a wedding. Most professional videographers will aim to have two cameras in church to get a **good range** of close-ups and 'whole congregation' shots.

> *What about sound?*
> A professional videographer can make sure the sound is captured **without interfering** with the church's PA system.

Customization

The very word 'customization' can worry faithful clergy. Likewise, having any service that is 'client based' is a challenge to us, for the very reason that we bring something to that experience, as does God himself. Worship, though, is both a subjective and an objective exercise. Couples tell us that making the service their own is a key factor in being delighted with the occasion. Their sense of ownership and uniqueness is directly linked to the extent to which the liturgical minister has allowed and enabled their influence to work within the liturgy. Moreover, couples are more likely to stay with the church community if they have a greater sense of ownership in the one moment that has been 'theirs' in the life of the worshipping community. Obviously, this does not mean that clergy should accede to every wacky request but it does mean that clergy need to remember at all times, 'whose service it is' in the sight of God. If we hope weddings take place only once, then we have a duty to ensure that each couple are not only asked for their contribution but led into discovering what is the right expression of their love for each other in church.

Common Worship provides a structure for the marriage liturgy and there are, of course, certain legal points to maintain as standard. But in recent times, we have become used to funerals becoming more flexible and participatory, and so perhaps weddings should follow this example. The liturgical structure is meant to enable freedom within worship norms. We ought to be enthusiastic about such possibilities and help couples express, what after all, is a celebration of love.

I spoke to Tim Sledge, Vicar of Romsey Abbey. He told me how he had found that involving the wider wedding group in the liturgy had borne fruit. In the preparations for one wedding, he had noticed that this was a big deal for the mother of the bride – it really mattered to her. His pastoral heart noticed that the Mum was finding the liturgical preparations difficult, not in the interfering 'mother of the bride' way, but at a spiritual level. Taking her to one side and talking it through, he found that Mum would be best helped by having a more active role in the service and that the couple were very open to that idea. For Mum, there was a need to be involved in the action of 'giving away' and Tim explained how the liturgy allowed for this. Similarly, another Mum had found it helpful to read a lesson. Both had expressed their gratitude, and more than that, it had had an impact on them and they were now far more open to discovering what church was all about. This is using the liturgy to do its transforming job, and not just for the couple but for all those participating.

On a much lighter note, the wedding I took last Saturday was the first that I had ever experienced with – bubbles. Yes, bubbles. Having noted our prohibition for confetti, the couple had decided to use bubbles to send them on their way. They found you can buy this in containers shaped like champagne bottles from a wedding company (more evidence of the world of weddings today). As they left the Lady Chapel, the congregation blew bubbles to send them on their way, inside and outside of church. Instead of being twee it was incredibly moving and gave me the opportunity to preach about our prayers supporting those being married and rising to heaven. Personalization can be a wonderful thing and can contribute towards the liturgy – if we but allow it.

7

Marriage as mission

So, what next? Let's face it, some of the clergy and parishes of the Church of England are not the most elastic when it comes to change. There is often a good reason for this as those in parish ministry engage with the constraints of everyday reality and recognize that real progress takes time and effort. Any new initiatives need to be proved worthy of investment. Also, importantly, and however it may seem otherwise, we believe in consensus. The changes in marriage law in recent times have proved to be a challenge for the Church and so in time-honoured way, it has taken us ages to respond. But now that we have responded, we are a force to be reckoned with, so the 'best of the rest' in the wedding business had better look out! With the new marriage legislation, a new chapter begins, and if it is accompanied by a real heart and commitment to mission, we cannot fail. And for once, the change has come from the Church as an organization, rather than just from the bottom up.

As we covered in Chapter 3, despite the brave new world of weddings, exotic locations and consumer choice, many people still see getting married in church as being the best way to be married 'properly'. Goodwill is still on our side and the Church has responded. The previous, long-standing system of marriage qualification has not been changed but has been added to with a more flexible scheme of connections. Rules are designed for mission rather than malfunction. It is not a free for all, yet the mobile reality of life today is honoured and recognized. On top of that, the Archbishops' Council is investing in helping the Church nationally to do weddings better. The Weddings Project has been set up and will be producing material in the future. So what are we waiting for?

There has been a problem, the Church has recognized that problem, has done something about it, changed the law, put in place a staff team and resources and a national initiative. The only thing that can stand in the way of progress is the clergy and the parishes – so let's do something about it!

Let me give you an example. She won't thank me for this, but here goes. Katie is my daughter. At the time of writing she is doing her AS level revision and has just started to learn to drive. In a year she'll be leaving us for university and my world will fall apart (don't let her know I said that). Even now, at 17 years of age, under the new legislation, she qualifies to be married in five places: three parish churches, one abbey and one cathedral. She doesn't know who she wants to marry yet but by the time that she does, we shall probably be able to add two or three more places to that list, when she moves on to university and work and her parents have moved again. To say that just because her first post-university flat is within a particular parish boundary, and that if she falls in love and wants to get married, she's got to be married *there* is, well, ludicrous. That's not going to keep her coming to church and she'll only move again in time anyway. Far better that she is able to consider her options with her (still hypothetical) fiancé and feel that the Church is on her side and welcoming her somewhere special rather than the very real possibility that she is put off church for ever by some grumpy vicar who simply wants to talk about parish boundaries and fees. God has provided a new way forward for us, and we should embrace it with all the enthusiasm we can muster. Katie ought to be married wherever she has a qualifying or special connection. Let's celebrate the fact that she might want to get married in church at all – especially having had to suffer living in a vicarage, which is enough to put her off for life! The new legislation and its accompanying mission opportunities provide a new way forward for every priest, every couple and every parish, and for Katie. And there are thousands of Katies out there, eager to be married in church.

So what more do we want as evidence for the way in which we should work? Here is a new opportunity and responsibility and it starts with each and every priest.

The priestly responsibility

The first thing for us all, as priests who will be taking weddings in the new legal environment, is to be sure that we all see marriage for its mission possibilities, both for the couple and for the Church. For the couple, getting married in church is a chance to respond more fully to God's call and to discover more about him in their lives. Couples actually *want* to engage with God through the Church, which is the main reason why most of them contact the Church in the first place. Through enjoyable engagement with them and through marriage preparation there is a real opportunity for growth and this needs to be led and managed by the priest who will marry them. Challenging couples into a deeper relationship with Christ often comes as a welcome surprise to them. Nearly half of our adult confirmation classes at St Albans for the last four years have been made up from wedding couples.

Similarly, getting married in church is a mission opportunity for the Church and an opportunity to share the good news, a chance to meet people where they are and to help them move to a new place that is closer to God. So we should not be making all this effort around weddings solely because of falling numbers (although, of course, more Christians would be a good idea), but because we believe in marriage and its place within society and the Church. The priest needs to have this outlook. A wedding in church is an important life event both for the couple and for the Church. Life events need our ministry and our total commitment. So the clergy need to have the clear priority that weddings are important and require all our professional resources.

While it's clear that the Church is not in the wedding business for itself, there can be benefits for those open to mission. A priest told me about their need for a buildings expert to help with faculty applications. They advertised in the Sunday notices, not confident of any takers. A positive response came from a bride to be, attending church in the run-up to a wedding. In short order, the bride came on to

> the PCC and has provided lots of good advice, as well as
> bringing her 'un-churched' husband to church. God works
> in mysterious ways, even through faculty legislation!

If that mindset is in place, training, especially in working the new legislation, will be important. Each diocese ought to be offering training in this area. But be sure that this training is not just about legalities but also about the mission opportunities and responsibilities of marriage too. It sounds obvious, but make the legislation and your parish policy around marriage your friend, a subject you know back to front so that you can give advice the moment a request comes to you.

The next task is to review the way in which each priest provides marriage in church. Often we learn our trade from curacy days and the quality of that training can be mixed. Opportunities for taking weddings may have been limited. Clergy are not very good at asking for help for fear of showing ignorance, but help is regularly needed in engaging with couples and in leading wedding services. One way forward is to meet with a friend to talk over how each of you does the whole wedding thing and to learn from each other's experience. This kind of 'buddy' system works because of the trust involved and because it often confirms good practice rather than just points out shortcomings. Having confirmation that you are doing something in the right way can be just as valuable as learning something new, especially when clergy frequently minister in isolation. Become familiar with the Church of England web site and other resources such as Transforming Worship (www.transformingworship.org.uk). Make time to visit another parish for a wedding to see how others do things. All too often clergy only attend services that they are taking themselves. Make developing your 'wedding performance' a training priority for the coming year.

Parochial preparation

The preparation of the parish to celebrate marriage is intertwined with the professionalism of the priest. Each and every parish where weddings may take place needs to develop a new marriage mission policy as the new legislation comes into use. There are a number of phases and decisions that need to be worked through with parish staff, churchwardens and the parochial church council.

- Discover how much the PCC members know about weddings in the parish. It is often surprising how little is known about rules of qualification, parish boundaries and parish policy.

- Invite along the parish organist, verger, flower arranger as applicable.

- Inform the PCC about the changes to the law and the implications for the parish or team.

- Explain the reasons behind the legislative change and the opportunity for mission.

- Look with fresh eyes at how weddings come to the parish. How are enquiries generally made? Is the parish passive in encouraging marriages or inundated with requests? What does the parish do to encourage weddings in church and what more can be done?

- Discuss whether weddings are seen as a joyful opportunity or a time-consuming inconvenience.

- Is the advice given regarding wedding choices (e.g. bells, videos etc.) generally positive in description or negative? Is the prevailing culture 'what you can't do in St Agatha's' or 'this works best in St Agatha's and is our agreed parish policy for a great wedding'? What is your parish ethos towards weddings – 'No, you can't' or 'Yes, you can.'?

- What is provided in your parish for marriage preparation?

- How can the PCC help the minister in the provision of weddings in church? Can help be provided through marriage preparation, practical help on the day and follow up?

- How can the congregation welcome and value those coming to the church for marriage, especially when they come to hear banns being read?

- What other congregational groups and nurture programmes are available to the couple?

- Review the information provided for couples, especially printed details. Perhaps a leaflet can be produced listing the parish policy regarding weddings and the content choices couples can make. Read this material from their perspective, from a 'client' viewpoint. Information can include practical details such as where cars are best parked and what ushers do, but also liturgical guidance, such as the choir's repertoire or suggested readings. Fees should also be agreed and easily identified.

- A policy needs to be made over the date of payment of fees, and ideally one invoice prepared by the parish treasurer and settled in advance. Again, this process can be both explained by the minister and printed in any helpful leaflet.

- Ensure any printed material looks as professional as possible; everything else to do with weddings will be posh.

- Agree a policy over printed Orders of Service. For example, if a couple are having a printed order of service, it ought to include the Pastoral Introduction to be read by the people before the service begins. One couple I married recently also included a brief history of the church and its spiritual use today – it worked really well and has become a standard text available to others.

- Couples tend to keep everything to do with their wedding day, so provide a 'change of address' slip for when they move house.

- Agree post-wedding ministry such as first anniversary card or phone call and any subsequent gatherings. Invite the couple to church on their anniversary and welcome them. Invite wedding couples to targeted social occasions or services.

- Be sure to be familiar with other liturgical possibilities such as a Dedication after a Civil Marriage and Thanksgiving for Marriage.

- Review all the above annually.

Wider preparations

The deanery needs to play an increasing role in the provision of weddings in each locality. First, there should be a discussion in deanery chapter about the Marriage Measure and any implications of a particularly local nature. The rural dean needs to take a leading role in encouraging clergy to work together both in administering the new legislation and in celebrating weddings. This may be especially true where there are so-called 'pretty churches' where weddings may be in greater demand than in other places. Clergy will have to become more willing to work together through such issues, for the good of the whole Church. Sharing in the liturgical celebration of a wedding must become more general practice.

Each diocese should provide training for clergy, not just regarding the new legislation but in celebrating weddings in church. Incumbents who train curates should receive training themselves to be sure that what they are passing on is best practice within their setting. The Diocesan Liturgical Committee may be able to help in this area but encouragement from the bishop will also help. Archdeacons may like to include weddings in their articles of enquiry to see if parishes have reviewed their practice and policy. Each diocese may like to look at how weddings are promoted in their locality.

Challenges and concerns

There seem to be four main challenges and concerns arising from the new legislation and its possibilities.

What if the parish is inundated by weddings? How can we manage the time and administration?

This would be a happy problem to have and an unlikely one in most parishes. Those parish churches that will attract a lot of weddings will need to re-evaluate this area of ministry. It should not be seen as an imposition but as a specialization of a particular parish and in time, clergy appointments will need to reflect this emphasis. There is an analogy with secondary education. All schools are schools but most secondary schools have some form of specialist status. This could apply to these types of parish and they can become centres of effective marriage ministry and mission. Resources may need to be widened and shared with others. Parishes that are very busy may be helped by reaching out to others for support – within the local cluster, deanery and diocese.

So-called 'pretty' churches will get all the weddings and less beautiful settings will have fewer weddings.

This happens already. My last church was nothing to look at from the outside but a gem on the inside. But under the previous marriage law, we never felt able to promote weddings in church. When people did get across the threshold, we kept them. All parishes need to become more effective in selling themselves. Clergy may also be able to take a wedding in another church to maintain the pastoral link. The principle of qualifying connection is important whether a church is pretty or not and it needs to be honoured.

The Marriage Measure is too much of a free for all and will devalue marriage in church.

All the research shows us that a church wedding is still really important and is seen as such by the majority of people. The problem has been not of too much marriage in church but too little. We cannot encourage marriage itself if we do not have contact with people. The Church needs open doors for those seeking to commend their love to God. The responsibility rests with priest and parishes to ensure weddings are celebrated in a serious, nurturing and welcoming way so that each and every couple can look back on their experience in church as the crowning of both their love and their great day. Nothing will devalue marriage more than not having weddings in church. Marriage is a mission moment.

The clergy don't really want more weddings because of the time involved and the less than obvious return in terms of regular commitment.

In these days of fewer clergy more thinly spread this is not simply a negative comment, it is a realistic challenge – another straw on the camel's back. But we will not solve the Church's problems by being fearful of the future. The clergy above all need to be confident in the message of the gospel, hopeful for the mission of the Church, and proud of the value of Christian marriage.

I am reminded of the old joke about the man of faith. Floods came and swamped his house. He had to retreat upstairs for downstairs was waterlogged. The police came to rescue him but he declined their help saying, 'It's all right, God will provide!' The flood waters rose and he had to retreat onto the roof. The RNLI came to rescue him but he declined their help saying; 'It's all right, God will provide!' The floods rose still further and the man had to stand on the chimney top. The RAF sent a helicopter to rescue him but he sent them away saying, 'It's all right, God will provide!' The man was beginning to drown as the emergency services looked on. He prayed, 'Lord, save me, why have you not provided for me?' A booming voice from heaven was heard to say, 'Look my son, I've provided the police, the RNLI and the RAF, what more do you need?' God has provided for us new legislation, a new mission heart and support from central church resources – its time we learnt to swim again.

The Weddings Project

The launch of the Marriage Measure is the focus for a project initiated by the Archbishops' Council, tasked to develop new ideas that could go on to support the whole Church in its marriage ministry.

The Weddings Project is a two-year venture, working in Bradford and Oxford Dioceses and two Cambridge theological colleges.

The project team has been listening carefully to 176 clergy in consultations in the trial zones, and 411 engaged and newly married couples. They have also quizzed 1,800 brides to be at the National Wedding Shows and polled the wider public. From this, they have developed 'a three-way approach to resourcing and encouraging churches through the latest research, marketing and deeper theological reimagining'.

The Weddings Project aims to attract more people for a wedding, develop an explicit public advocacy for marriage and articulate an approach to mission that works well with the Measure.

Watch out for news from the Weddings Project. I commend this work wholeheartedly.

8

The last word . . .

Jamie's experience

This chapter begins and ends with real-life stories.

Jamie spoke to a priest he knew, concerned about what to do following a visit to his parish priest. He'd been to visit his vicar to enquire about marriage. Jamie is a bit alternative, a 'goth' all dressed in black. With his girlfriend, they had approached the village church with a mixture of hope and hesitation. After a little while, the vicar asked them why they wanted to be married in church. Jamie replied that he'd wanted to give his bride the best wedding, at a fancy stately home, but he couldn't afford it. The vicar replied that that was not a good reason for getting married in church, and they ought to think about what they really wanted. The couple were crestfallen. While the priest may have been right in challenging the motives, he had missed the point. The prevailing culture around weddings (where we started) meant Jamie had a different starting place in his make-up. Now that he had come to the Church, here was an opportunity to be grasped not scorned. This first contact was crucial for Jamie and his bride, and for the Church.

The Marriage Measure 2008 challenges us all to welcome the Jamies of this world with God's love in abundance. We believe in marriage, now we have the framework to celebrate it more effectively and more wonderfully. I believe it is what God wants from us.

Good news

Did you know?

- Half the population goes to church or a chapel in a year for a wedding.

- 53 per cent of the population say church weddings feel more 'proper'.

- The Church of England still marries 57,000 couples a year, which is 22 per cent of the marrying population.

- All church weddings account for 33 per cent of the whole.

- 9 out of 10 newly-weds say marriage makes them happier.

- 9 out of 10 newly-weds say marriage improved their relationship.

The fact that the Church of England has such a key role in weddings is really good news. We need to celebrate this and proclaim it anew. It's a confidence thing. We have a unique resource and tradition and a cherished place in society. The people are on our side and God is with us. I would headline these essential points to help us be more effective in celebrating the wonder of marriage in weddings.

- First contact is crucially important.

- People are attracted by the venue, the vows and the vicar.

- Personal relationship with the priest is precious.

- Marriage preparation is best focused on the service itself.

- Couples come to us with a deep spiritual awareness ready to be deepened still further.

- The liturgy can and should be transforming.

- We have a lot to learn about follow-up.

These are the essential points about weddings in church today. Each and every parish needs to focus on these things and make weddings 'good news' for the souls in their care. The last word ought to go to a real bride, who experienced good news in her marriage and this is good news for the Church. At the time of writing, their first child has just been born and the baptism has been booked!

Andrea writes about her wedding to Mark

Why marriage for us?
Why not?! Something I always knew I was going to do from a very young age, (apart from the compulsory Women's Lib stage when I was about 19 years old). I never craved nor looked for marriage; independent and ambitious, loving family, wonderful friends and quite frankly living a very hedonistic lifestyle.

I met Mark one night through a mutual friend. I now realize that 'love' at first sight really does exist, and that's coming from a cynic. I floated home that night, knowing that something 'weird' had happened to me and we hadn't even exchanged phone numbers! I realized I felt alive again. All Mark remembers is meeting me that night and thinking 'Blimey, my old lines aren't going to work on this one, I'll have to try a little harder' . . . and luckily he did. Two hedonists in no great hurry – but from day one of our relationship I just knew we were heading towards the ultimate goal of spending the rest of our lives together and to both of us that meant marriage.

We never really discussed marriage in our two-year dating period – I'm very old fashioned in the sense I want the man to be 100 per cent sure this is what HE wants, not something he feels obligated to do because his girlfriend's impatient, in need of a big party, broody, watching all her mates doing it and so on. So we never discussed it. We were totally secure with one another so there was no need. Then one night while watching the sun set over the Nevada Desert and supping happily away at my margarita, Mark dragged me off to one side, got down on one knee and proposed. Everything came crashing in on me – elation, fear, more 'weirdness', inexplicable feelings and through the tears (of joy) I managed to mumble 'yes', then the engagement ring came out and I knew I'd made the right decision! Then nothing. Nothing for a long time. We just wanted to enjoy the time of being engaged. No hassle, no running around trying to book the venue or try on dresses. We were just enjoying the 'we're engaged period'. Sadly, I'd witnessed friends get so caught up in the wedding planning, they'd forgotten to ask the all important question – 'Do I *really* want to marry this man or am I just in love with the dream of having a great wedding?' I thought about nothing else for the first year and truth be known, of course, on certain days when he'd upset me, I did reconsider! But something was different with Mark, when I fought with him. My gut reaction was always, 'How can we resolve this issue?' as opposed to previous relationships when all that used to go through my head was 'How do I have the strength to walk away from this man?' Mark was always going to be larger than life and that is also what attracted me to him in the first place, so when the calm came over me, it was full steam ahead for the bash of the decade!

Why a religious ceremony?
In my early adult life I'd done the agnostic, atheist and downright self-indulgent stages; anything that was cool at the time, but the strangest thing was I always knew I would never marry anywhere other than in a church. The two go hand in hand in my view. If I were to have a civil ceremony, it would signify a business relationship with my partner, not a marriage. It's a strictly personal preference, and I have been to many a friend's civil wedding; but it always left me cold, because there was 'someone' missing from the proceedings. That 'someone' was God. So on the day of our wedding there were three persons involved, not two. Mark, myself

and the priest. But it didn't hit me until quite late on how important this was: our vicar was the 'bridge' between us and the sanctity of marriage. Without him or the church I simply wouldn't have felt married, just 'legally attached'.

I've lost far more people to death than I should have for my years and another wonderful comfort of having a church wedding was that I knew 'they' would all be there with us; everyone Mark and I had ever loved would be together under one roof – because, as childish or strange as it seemed, they knew where to come, there was this one building that united us all, and the calm I'd come to welcome over the past year of going to the church made me really believe that somehow this was all channelled 'spiritually' so we could all be together. I never once cried on my wedding day for the people I'd lost, because I knew they were there and knew where to find us.

Why in church?

This was never really in question for Mark and me . . . we just had to convince the vicar. Mark was christened there, as was his older brother and both went to the church school. Mark, however, hardly went in the church for about 20 years; it was like the old neighbour that you pass everyday and say 'hi' to but keep on walking. He loved the church and was immensely proud of it, always pointing it out to me whenever we were driving back into town – whichever part of town we were driving into, he'd tell me that I could see the church tower if I looked, left, right or straight ahead; it was a part of him and I realized this ran deeper than I'd originally thought. Mark's brother was also married at the parish church along with many of our friends. There was nowhere else Mark wanted to get married and, of course, when I'd moved up to be with Mark, the church was an instant hit with me! But we didn't live in the parish.

I wanted the parish church for all the vacuous, 'bridey' reasons, of course: romantic, beautiful, historic, none of my mates had done it in here before . . . the list is endless on the 'reasons for getting married in this particular church'. BUT, I'm pleased to report, that changed. The vicar encouraged us to come along to the Sunday services, and so we did, and we found it more rewarding than we thought, even for a Sunday morning!

Getting married in the church we wanted

Sadly for Mark and the vicar, I'm a bit of a perfectionist, so everything had to be perfect at the church service. I wanted every second to count and to mean something. Again I'd been to so many weddings where the vicar is just going through the motions, but I've never held the vicars responsible for this. Basically, you get out what you put in. This is why it was so great having gone to the church for a year before we got married. I wasn't walking down the aisle to a stranger, I was walking down the aisle to somebody I knew and by that point, the vicar had no choice but to know me, as I'd sent him that many emails. This made a huge difference to the ceremony. It made every word have meaning, like I was hearing the vows for the first time. Our priest injected his own humour throughout the service, normally at my expense, but seeing how I'd set myself up so nicely it was bound to happen! It was a true, true celebration. He knew us and we knew him, so everything felt so natural and fun, combined with a real sense of ceremony. Towards the end of the service the vicar cracked a joke about the collection tray, the roar of laughter that flew down the aisle hit me like a tonne of bricks. It was actually physical and I hope I never ever lose that feeling. All that warmth and jollity coming from the congregation and flying around the three of us was nothing short of magical and was one of the highlights of the day.

People were buzzing when they came out of the church; every single person came up to Mark and me and (after they'd complimented the dress, of course), told us that was the best wedding service they'd ever been to. Curiously most people said 'If only church were like that every Sunday, then I'd go.' I did say that Sunday services were actually injected with humour and 'real life' in the parish, but I guess like most people, its years since most have frequented any church.

I know the vicar had pulled out all the stops for us, it was even supposed to be his day off, but nothing was wasted on me; I felt every second of it and it really was the best day of my life. The most interesting transition for me was going from sleepless nights worrying if my napkins would match my chair tie-backs, to suddenly a week before the big day going completely calm; the tie-backs didn't matter and indeed I probably would have to let out my corset to allow myself to breathe after dinner, thus losing the 24-inch waist . . . none of it mattered, I just wanted to get married. I just wanted to walk down the aisle, pick Mark up on the way and go and be married by the priest we had come to know as a spiritual friend.

Post wedding day

We've been married almost three years now, with our first child en route, which both of us are utterly thrilled about. We can't wait to have him or her baptized in the place where we were married and where Mark was baptized also. People still talk about our wedding day with such high regard and I think that really helps on the days when Mark and I don't see eye to eye! I think back to that day and what it all really means. Yes we could go to church more frequently, but most weekends I either work or go to my parents; but our parish church is a part of us now, and that's a very calming feeling. It's not the old neighbour we walk past anymore; we stop and go in, and I finally realize that in the hectic lifestyle we lead, we're not doing the old neighbour a favour; it's actually the other way round!

Appendix 1

Church of England Marriage Measure 2008

A Measure passed by the General Synod of the Church of England to enable persons to be married in a place of worship in a parish with which they have a qualifying connection; and for connected purposes. [22 May 2008]

Be it enacted by the Queen's most Excellent Majesty, by and with the advice and consent of the Lords Spiritual and Temporal, and Commons, in this present Parliament assembled, and by the authority of the same, as follows:

1 Marriages solemnized in churches, etc. in parishes with which a party has a qualifying connection

1. A person intending to be married shall have the like, but no greater, right to have the marriage solemnized in a parish church of a parish with which he or she has a connection specified in subsection (3) below (in this Measure referred to as a 'qualifying connection') as that person has to have the marriage solemnized in the parish church of the parish in which he or she resides or which is his or her usual place of worship.

2. Where a church or other building licensed for public worship has been designated, under section 29(2) of the Pastoral Measure 1983 (1983 No. 1), as a parish centre of worship, this section shall apply to such centre of worship, while the designation is in force, as it applies to a parish church.

3. For the purposes of this section a person has a qualifying connection with a parish in which the marriage is to be solemnized if –

    a. that person was baptized in that parish (unless the baptism took place in a combined rite which included baptism and confirmation) or is a person whose confirmation has been entered in the register book of confirmation for any church or chapel in that parish;

    b. that person has at any time had his or her usual place of residence in that parish for a period of not less than six months;

    c. that person has at any time habitually attended public worship in that parish for a period of not less than six months;

    d. a parent of that person has during the lifetime of that person had his or her usual place of residence in that parish for a period of not less than six months or habitually attended public worship in that parish for that period; or

    e. a parent or grandparent of that person has been married in that parish.

4. For the purpose of subsection (3)(d) or (e) above 'parent' includes an adoptive parent and any other person who has undertaken the care and upbringing of the person seeking to establish a qualifying connection and 'grandparent' shall be construed accordingly.

5. A person who has the right to have a marriage solemnized in accordance with subsection (1) above shall have the like right to have the banns of that marriage published in the parish church where the marriage is to be solemnized.

6. The right to have banns published conferred by subsection (5) above is additional to and not in substitution for the requirements

of section 6 of the 1949 Act for banns to be published in the parish church of the parish where the parties to the marriage reside or of each parish in which one of them resides.

7. Where a marriage is intended to be solemnized in accordance with subsection (1) above following the publication of banns by virtue of subsection (5) above section 11(2) and (4) of the 1949 Act shall apply as those subsections apply to a marriage of which the banns have been published in a parish or district in which neither of the persons to be married resides by virtue of section 6(4) of that Act.

8. Subject to subsection (9) below, a person who wishes to have his or her marriage solemnized in accordance with subsection (1) above shall provide such information, written or otherwise, as the minister of the parish in which the marriage is to be solemnized may require in order to satisfy himself or herself that that person has a qualifying connection and –

   a. section 8 of the 1949 Act shall apply as if the reference in that section to a clergyman were a reference to the minister, and

   b. the minister shall be under a duty, when considering whether any information provided to him or her is sufficient to satisfy himself or herself under this subsection that the person wishing to have the marriage solemnized has a qualifying connection, to have regard to any guidance issued under section 3 below.

9. If the minister considers that it is necessary to do so, in order to satisfy himself or herself that a person has a qualifying connection, he or she may require that person to supply or support any information required to be provided under subsection (8) above by means of a statutory declaration.

10. Where a public chapel is licensed by a bishop for the publication of banns and the solemnization of marriages under section 20 of

the 1949 Act, this section shall apply as if that chapel were a parish church of the parish or of any parish the whole or part of which is within the district specified in the licence.

11. In this section 'church' does not include a cathedral.

12. In this section –

   a. 'minister' means –

      i. where a special cure of souls has been assigned to any priest for the area in which the church where the marriage is to be solemnized is situated, whether in a team ministry or otherwise,

      that priest, or

      ii. where sub-paragraph (i) above does not apply, the incumbent of the benefice in the area of which that church is situated, or

      iii. where neither of the above sub-paragraphs applies, the priest-in-charge of that benefice, or

      iv. where none of the above sub-paragraphs applies, in the case of a team ministry, the vicar, if any, appointed by the bishop to act as rector under section 20(14) of the Pastoral Measure 1983 (1983 No. 1) or, if there is no such vicar appointed, the vicar who has held office for the longest period in that ministry, or

      v. where none of the above sub-paragraphs applies, the rural dean of the deanery in which that church is situated;

   b. 'parish' includes a conventional district; and

   c. any reference to baptism, confirmation, marriage or public worship shall be construed as a reference to baptism, confirmation, marriage or public worship, as the case may be, according to the rites of the Church of England.

13.   Where, as a result of a pastoral scheme or otherwise, a parish has ceased to exist or the boundaries thereof have been altered and a person who wishes to have his or her marriage solemnized in accordance with subsection (1) above can establish a qualifying connection with a place situated within such a parish then, if that place is, at the time when the notice under section 8 of the 1949 Act is delivered, situated within the parish in which the church where the marriage is to be solemnized is situated, that person shall be deemed to have a qualifying connection with that parish.

14.   In relation to the establishment of a qualifying connection under subsection (3)(a) above by virtue of confirmation the references in subsection (13) above to a place shall be construed as a reference to the church or other place of worship in whose register the confirmation was entered.

2 Marriage by common licence

1.   Notwithstanding section 15 of the 1949 Act a common licence may be granted to a person for the solemnization of a marriage in any church or chapel in which that person may be married under section 1 above and section 16(1)(b) of that Act shall, where a common licence may be granted by virtue of this section, have effect as if it required one of the persons to be married to swear that one or both of those persons has a qualifying connection with a parish within the meaning of section 1(3) above and to state the nature of that connection and section 1(8) above shall apply as if the reference therein to the minister of the parish were a reference to the authority having power to grant the licence.

2.   Where an application has been made for the grant of a common licence under subsection (1) above section 1(13) above shall

have effect as if the reference to the date on which the notice required under section 8 of the 1949 Act is delivered were a reference to the date of the application for the grant of the common licence.

3 Guidance

The House of Bishops shall from time to time issue guidance as to the exercise of any functions by a minister under section 1(8) or (9) above or by the authority having power to grant a common licence under section 1(8) as applied by section 2 above.

4 Supplementary provisions

1. In this Measure 'the 1949 Act' means the Marriage Act 1949 (12, 13 & 14 Geo 6 c. 76) and, unless the context otherwise requires, expressions used in this Measure have the same meaning as in the 1949 Act.

2. Where a marriage has been solemnized –

    a. in accordance with section 1(1) above, or

    b. on the authority of a common licence granted by virtue of section 2 above, it shall not be necessary in support of the marriage to give any proof that either party had a qualifying connection with the parish in which the marriage was solemnized and no evidence shall be given to prove the contrary in any proceedings touching the validity of the marriage.

5 Citation, commencement and extent

1. This Measure may be cited as the Church of England Marriage Measure 2008.

2. This Measure shall come into force on such day as the

Archbishops of Canterbury and York may jointly appoint and different days may be appointed for different provisions.

3. This Measure shall extend to the whole of the provinces of Canterbury and York except the Channel Islands and the Isle of Man, except that the provisions thereof may be extended to the Channel Islands as defined in the Channel Islands (Church Legislation) Measures 1931 and 1957 or either of them, in accordance with those Measures, and, if an Act of Tynwald or an instrument made under an Act of Tynwald so provides, shall extend to the Isle of Man subject to such exceptions, adaptions or modifications as may be specified in the Act of Tynwald or instrument.

Appendix 2: Sample application form

PARISH OF

CHURCH OF ENGLAND MARRIAGE MEASURE 2008

Form for completion by a person who wishes to marry in the parish by virtue of a Qualifying Connection with the parish

A Warm Welcome – We are delighted that you wish to marry here.

The Minister of the parish, whose name and address are set out below, is under a legal duty to be satisfied that you can lawfully marry in the parish before the marriage can take place or a firm date and time can be fixed for it. To make this process as quick and simple as possible, whichever of you claims to have a connection with the parish is asked to complete this form and return it to the Minister.

PLEASE BEGIN BY READING THE FOLLOWING NOTES:

1.   Please complete all four parts (A, B, C and D. In Part D please complete sections 1 and 2 and the question(s) in section 3 which apply to you.

2.   Before completing the form, and in particular Part D, you may well find it helpful to read the material on the Church of England Marriage Measure 2008 on the Church of England web site at www.cofe.anglican.org including the House of Bishops' Guidance on the Measure. If you do not have access to the Internet the

parish will be pleased to send you a copy of an explanatory leaflet and the House of Bishops' Guidance.

3.   If you are not certain about how to complete any part of the form, please contact the parish for advice.

4.   If

   - either of you has been married previously, and your former husband or wife is still alive; or

   - either of you is not a UK national;

please alert the Minister to that as soon as possible, even before submitting the completed form, so that the special issues that arise can be considered without delay.

5.   When the Minister has considered the completed form, it is possible that the Minister may still need to ask you for some further documents or other information, or may need to ask someone holding an official position in the parish for further information in support of your connection with the parish. If any special issue arises in your case it is also possible that the Minister may need to ask for advice on it from the diocesan legal adviser. However, if any of these becomes necessary, the Minister will see that you are kept fully informed.

The Minister of the Parish is ....

PART A – REQUEST TO MARRY IN PARISH

Person completing form – please insert full names of yourself and your fiancé(e)

I, ..., wish to be married to .... according to the rites of the Church of England in the Parish of ....by virtue of my having a qualifying connection with the parish under the Church of England (Marriage Measure 2008).

I confirm that the information and answers given in and supplied with this form are correct to the best of my knowledge and belief.

Signed ....

Date ....

PART B – THE PROPOSED MARRIAGE

My fiancé(e) and I wish to be married in the following church/place of worship in the parish of ....

Or My fiancé(e) and I wish to be married in the parish church of the parish of ....

Our preferred date and time for the marriage would be*

....

....

* Please see introductory paragraph on page 1.

PART C – GENERAL INFORMATION ABOUT YOURSELF AND YOUR FIANCÉ(E)

(Please complete in block capitals)

BRIDE – Full name

Present home address

Tel (day)

Tel (evening)

Tel (mobile)

Email

Date of birth

Nationality

BRIDEGROOM – Full name

Present home address

Tel (day)

Tel (evening)

Tel (mobile)

Email

Date of birth

Nationality

Have either of you previously been married?   Yes/No

If yes,

(a)   When did the marriage end? *(Give date)*

(b)   How did it end? *e.g. divorce, death*

(c)   Is the other spouse still alive?

Note: The law also forbids a person who has entered into a civil partnership to enter into a marriage while the civil partnership is still subsisting.

Are you and your fiancé(e) related by marriage?   Yes/No

Are you and your fiancé(e) connected by marriage? Yes/No

If your answer is yes to either of these questions please give details.

PART D – YOUR QUALIFYING CONNECTION WITH THE PARISH
Please complete sections 1 and 2 and whichever question(s) in section 3 apply

SECTION 1 *Please tick relevant statement(s)*

I wish to rely on a connection with the parish by virtue of **one or more** of the following:

- I was baptized in the parish (by a Church of England service/form of baptism)

- I have been confirmed (by a Church of England service) and my confirmation is entered in a register belonging to a church or chapel in the parish

- My parent or grandparent was married in the parish by a Church of England service

- I have had my usual place of residence in the parish for at least 6 months*

- My parent has had his or her usual place of residence in the parish for at least 6 months during my lifetime*

- I have habitually attended public worship at Church of England services in the parish for at least 6 months**

- My parent has habitually attended public worship at Church of England services in the parish for at least 6 months during my lifetime**

* *This can apply whether or not you or your parent(s) are still resident in the parish*

** *This can apply whether or not you or your parent(s) are still attending worship in the parish*

Note: In the Church of England Marriage Measure a parent means:

- *parent of either a legitimate or an illegitimate child; or*

- *an adoptive parent (This requires legal adoption); or*
- *a person 'who has undertaken the care and upbringing' of another person.*

For a grandparent one of the above three types of relationship must apply between each generation and the next, i.e. between the grandparent and the parent and between the parent and the person completing the form.

SECTION 2

Does any of the information on which you are relying to show your connection with the parish:

- give a name for you which is different from the one you have used on this form; or

- give the surname for any parent or grandparent of yours which is different from your surname as set out on this form?   Yes/No

If yes, please:

- give the previous/other name(s)

- explain how the difference has arisen and

- if the reason for the difference between the names is that you have changed your name, explain when and how the change(s) took place and provide any documentary information (e.g. adoption certificate, marriage certificate, deed poll for change of name).

PLEASE NOW GO ON TO COMPLETE THE PART(S) OF SECTION 3 THAT CORRESPOND TO THE STATEMENT(S) YOU HAVE TICKED IN SECTION 1 ABOVE

SECTION 3

Please answer the questions that relate to the connection(s) you have ticked in section 1.

Please give exact dates, places, names etc. if possible – if not, please give as much information as you can.

As regards what documentary or other information will be needed, please see the paragraphs in the House of Bishops' Guidance on the Church of England Marriage Measure (see front page) which deal with the relevant connection with the parish. The documents you supply will be returned to you.

Please complete your answer on a separate piece of paper if necessary and submit it with the form.

My Connection is that I was baptized in the parish (by a Church of England service/form of baptism)

When were you baptized?

Where were you baptized?

What documentary or other information do you have for this? *(Please submit any copy of an entry in the baptism register, baptism certificate or other documents with this form.)*

My connection is that I have been confirmed (by a Church of England service) and my confirmation is entered in a register belonging to a church or chapel in the parish

When were you confirmed?

Where were you confirmed?

Who prepared you for confirmation?

In which register is your confirmation recorded?

What documentary or other information do you have as regards the registration of your confirmation? *(Please submit any copy of an entry in the confirmation register, certificate etc. or other documents with this form.)*

My connection is that my parent or grandparent was married in the parish by a Church of England service

When and where did the marriage take place?

Please give names of the parties to the marriage, and state how the relevant party/parties are related to you.

What documentary or other information do you have for this? *(Please submit a copy of the relevant entry in the marriage register, marriage certificate or other documents with this form.)*

My connection is that I have had my usual place of residence in the parish for at least 6 months — *This can apply whether or not you are still resident in the parish*

Please give

- Each address at which you have been resident in the parish, and

- The dates between which that address was/has been your usual place of residence

What documentary or other information do you have for the above? *(Please submit the documents with this form.)*

My connection is that my parent has had his or her usual place of residence in the parish for at least 6 months during my lifetime – *This can apply whether or not your parent(s) is/are still resident in the parish*

Please give:

- Each address at which a parent of yours has been resident in the parish;

- The name(s) of the parent(s) resident there; and

- The dates between which that address is/was his/her/their usual place of residence

What documentary or other information do you have for the above? *(Please submit the documents with this form.)*

My connection is that I have habitually attended public worship at Church of England services in the parish for at least 6 months – *This can apply whether or not you are still attending worship in the parish*

When did you begin to attend public worship habitually in the parish?

If you no longer do so, when did you cease to do so?

Please state:

Where you worshipped in the parish during this period;

How often/on what occasions; and

What types of services you attended.

What documentary or other information do you have for the above? *(Please submit the documents with this form.)*

My connection is that my parent has habitually attended public worship at Church of England services in the parish for at least 6 months during my lifetime – *This can apply whether or not your parent(s) is/are are still attending worship in the parish*

When did your parent(s) begin to attend public worship habitually n the parish?

If that is no longer the case, when did it cease?

Please give his/her/their name(s) and his/her/their address(es) over that period.

Please state:

Where he/she/they worshipped in the parish during that period

How often/on what occasions; and

At what types of services?

What documentary or other information do you have for the above? *(Please submit the documents with this form.)*

Notes

1 *Common Worship: Pastoral Services*, Church House Publishing, 2000, 2005.

2 Henley Centre Headlight Vision March 2007, *Understanding Marriage, Weddings and Church Weddings*.

3 See *Report of Proceedings*, Vol. 38, No. 2, July 2007, p. 405.

4 Ipos Mori, national poll of adults 20 to 35 years of age for Civitas, May 2008.

5 Ipos Mori, national poll of adults 20 to 35 years of age for Civitas, May 2008.

6 ICM Research, national poll for Archbishops' Council, Church of England, April/May 2008.

7 Opinion Research Business, national poll for Archbishops' Council, Church of England, October 2007.

8 *Common Worship: Pastoral Services*, p. 136.

9 *Common Worship: Pastoral Services*, p. 120.

10 Andrew Body, *Growing Together*, Church House Publishing, 2005 and *Growing Together: The Course*, Church House Publishing, 2007.

11 Rowan Williams, April 2008, quoted on the Weddings Project web site: www.yourchurchwedding/your-marriage

12 Stephen Cottrell, Steven Croft, John Finney, Felicity Lawson and Robert Warren, *Emmaus: The Way of Faith series: Contact*, Church House Publishing, second edition, 2003; *Nurture*, Church House Publishing, 2003, *Growth: Growing as a Christian*, Church House Publishing, second edition, 2004; *Growth: Knowing God*, Church House Publishing, second edition, 2005; *Growth: Christian Lifestyle*, Church House Publishing, second edition, 2003.

13 Paul Bayes and Tim Sledge, *Mission-shaped Parish*, Church House Publishing, 2006.

14 The House of Bishops' Guidance is available at: www.cofe.anglican.org/info/socialpublic/marriagefamily/ marriageanddivorce/marriagemeasure/cemmguidance.pdf

15 Henley Centre Headlight Vision March 2007, *Understanding Marriage, Weddings and Church Weddings*.

16 *Common Worship: Pastoral Services*, p. 102.

17 The *Common Worship* separate booklet, *Marriage*, Church House Publishing, 2000.

18 The Series One rite is included in *Common Worship: Pastoral Services*, second edition, 2005.

19 There are other versions of these significant words, both in *The Book of Common Prayer* and in *Common Worship*.

General index

Index of biblical references